PRAISE FOR BROTHER VICTOR-ANTOINE

"*From a Monastery Kitchen* charms both palate and spirit."
—*FLORIDA TIMES-UNION*

"When the world is too much…,
retreat to *From a Monastery Kitchen* for food for the soul and the body."
—*BODY MIND SPIRIT MAGAZINE*

"These recipes guide you to hearty food that comes from the hand of God
to bless his people…laced with thought-provoking quotes
as the kitchen and chapel flavor each other."
—*CHRISTIANITY TODAY*

"The delectable recipes emphasize monastic values
of simplicity, frugality, and health."
—*RELIGIOUS STUDIES REVIEW*

"Brother Victor's recipes may well inspire all readers to live as
Saint Francis de Sales urges…'Let us strive to make the present moment beautiful.'"
—*NEW OXFORD REVIEW*

"Reading recipes was never so engaging—inspiring quotes
and informative notes are found on every page."
—*BOOKVIEWS*

From a Monastery Kitchen

THE CLASSIC NATURAL FOODS COOKBOOK

Brother Victor-Antoine d'Avila-Latourrette

Liguori/Triumph
LIGUORI, MISSOURI

Published by Liguori/Triumph
An imprint of Liguori Publications
Liguori, Missouri
www.liguori.org

Library of Congress Cataloging-in-Publication Data

D'Avila-Latourrette, Victor-Antoine.
    From a monastery kitchen / Victor-Antoine d' Avila Latourrette. —
Rev. ed.
      p. cm.
    Includes index.
    ISBN 978-0-7648-0850-0 (pbk.)
    1. Vegetarian cookery. 2. Monastic and religious life. 3. Quotations,
English. I. Title.

TX837.D25 1997
641.5'636—dc20   96–27482

Printed in the United States of America
18 17 16 15 14 / 13 12 11 10 9
Paperback edition 2002

Contents

Summer

Foreword

When our five children were small, some years ago, my morning trip to deliver them to their respective schools took us each day past a local monastery just at the hour when the monks were about in the garden. A few walked with heads bowed; others read their prayer books. The deep silence in the garden somehow penetrated our noisy car, and I never passed that spot without feeling joy.

A few years ago, while seeking a place of quiet retreat between conferences in New York City, I was led to Our Lady of the Resurrection Priory, then in Cold Spring, for a weekend of prayer. Many times since then I have journeyed up the Hudson River on the bumpy Poughkeepsie local to enter the life of prayer that Brother Victor-Antoine generously shares with those who come to the farmhouse monastery.

During the first visit I discovered something: Monasteries have kitchens, and monks have to cook. I had read about Brother Lawrence, the illiterate lay brother who practiced the presence of God in a monastery kitchen in seventeenth-century Europe, but I didn't know that the monks continued his practice in twenty-first century kitchens. Not only do monks have to cook, they have to wash dishes and do every kind of housekeeping chore. While they do not usually have young children to feed, they have many guests and must always be ready to set an extra place at the refectory table. As I visited other monasteries, I became aware of how hard our contemplative brothers and sisters work. Besides household chores, they farm and do craft work and make bread, cheese, or other items to sell. They work as hard as those of us "on the outside" because they, too, must make ends meet. Monasteries are largely self-supporting.

Since our contemplative brothers and sisters are vowed to a life of poverty, their kitchen work is often hard. Monasteries grow much of their own food, and young monks learn the art of food preservation. There are monks who are gifted cooks, like Brother Victor-Antoine, whose delicious simple meals, served in a spirit of deepest prayer, inspired the idea for this book. At Our Lady of the Resurrection Monastery, this gift for cooking is combined with a gift for frugality that chooses discarded food from supermarket trash bins and lovingly renders society's leavings edible. Brother Victor-Antoine also has a gift of song, and when he is not in the kitchen, he is sitting at a worktable writing and arranging music for the daily hours of prayer (Divine Office) in the chapel and for graces sung before meals. Praying, working, cooking, eating, singing, silence, and frugality—all these come together in the sacrament of the refectory.

Many of our monastic brothers and sisters come from farmer stock, like the rest of us, and monastery kitchens reflect the same double feast of body and spirit that the surrounding communities enjoy. Feast days, in fact, probably have always meant more in monasteries than anywhere else because of the sheer contrast with the disciplined asceticism of daily life. A monastic feast day is sober enough at that, but special foods are cooked with such care, special songs sung with such exaltation, that the whole monastery vibrates with holy joy. Holy feasting is not just a safety valve, however; it is a deep reaffirmation of the fact of Incarnation. The Son of Man came eating and drinking.

The cloister *is* very different from the outside world. If it were not, those of us who live in the world would not be drawn there. There is in the monastery a pointing of the whole life toward God, a drawing together of every activity into prayer. Again and again each day the monks return to the chapel, the very heart of every monastery, to lift up their hearts to God in silence, in word, and in song throughout the hours bounded by predawn vigils and evening prayers. These two offices, vigils and evening prayer, are like jeweled gates through which the monks move the world toward heaven every day of their lives.

This book was born in the kitchen of Our Lady of the Resurrection Priory. Having shared the joys of mealtime and even a little of the weariness of work with my monastic brothers and sisters, it came to me very strongly that this experience should and could be shared with other women and men. This book is intended to open the monastery door in a symbolic way for those who may never come here but who like to evoke the peace of the monastery in their own kitchens.

ELISE BOULDING

Introduction

It's been more than three decades since *From a Monastery Kitchen* was first presented to the public. Yet it seems like only yesterday that the book was being planned in the old kitchen of our former monastery in Cold Spring, a remote upstate region of New York. It found a steady readership, and even after a score of years we have received repeated requests for reprintings, both from American readers and from many in foreign countries. That a book endures the test of time is the most important test for an author.

This Liguori Publications edition is the first publication of the revised and expanded edition of the work in paperback, making it more widely available to the many people whose interest has never vanished—as indicated by the many letters that have come to the monastery in recent years.

Monastic cookery, as it has been practiced through the centuries, is cherished for its emphasis on simplicity, wholesome frugality, basic good taste, and the seasonal rhythms of the ingredients used. Monastic kitchens always strive for a healthy and balanced diet, fully aware from past experience that the monk and the nun must be properly nourished to serve God well. The human body is the temple of God, and its dietary needs must be respected.

Vegetables play a unique and most important role in the daily monastic fare, for all classic monastic diet throughout the ages has been predominantly vegetarian, while making provision for the inclusion of seafood and dairy products as well. Monastic gardeners make a point of cultivating extensive gardens that usually produce an adequate supply of vegetables, fruits, and herbs for daily culinary use.

Vegetarian cooking, for both health and spiritual reasons, has been rediscovered and has attained wide prominence. In the cooking at monasteries, this goes a long way toward sustaining and encouraging the positive trend we see today. Besides, a vegetarian meal—when well prepared and attractively presented at the monastic table—has a charm all its own. I am sure the same can be said of other vegetarian tables around the country and around the world.

And so, I am very happy that *From a Monastery Kitchen* is being given a wider audience in this revised and expanded paperback edition. I wish to thank our dear friend Elise Boulding, who was the originator of the idea of a monastic cookbook and who, with the first edition, started me on the then-unknown path of writing cookbooks. I have learned much since then; and I hope—with the help of God—to continue sharing with you the never-ending joys of monastic cooking.

BROTHER VICTOR-ANTOINE D'AVILA-LATOURRETTE

How to Use This Cookbook

This is a vegetarian cookbook; no meat recipes are included, but there are fish recipes. Not all monastics are vegetarian by any means, but the Rule of Saint Benedict, which Our Lady of the Resurrection Monastery follows, strongly encourages abstaining from meat. And each of us today must consider whether we want more than the least of us on the planet can have; most of our brothers and sisters do not have meat. Frugality takes many forms, and the way of simplicity that is most appropriate for any one household will be unique to that home.

If we were to reconstruct a typical monastic daily fare from the recipes that follow, it might be something like this: Breakfast would be simply coffee and one or two slices of bread. Lunch could include Lentil and Lemon Peel Soup, Tutti-Frutti Salad, Whole Wheat Buttermilk Bread, and tea. A supper menu might include Vegetable-Cheese Casserole, Stuffed Acorn Squash, Barrytown Apple Crumble, and tea.

The dinner table in a monastery is always set with care for both daily fare and feast days. Food is arranged to show the full beauty of God's harvest in vegetables, grains, dairy products, and fruit. Each night before the meal begins, the brothers or sisters of the order stand at their places around the candlelit table and sing grace. Then they quietly settle down to listening to the evening reading from Scripture or a classic religious writing while they eat. The delight in the fellowship of the table is always enhanced by one special ingredient added to every dish served: preparation with love.

The recipes that follow are arranged seasonally in order to link the great rhythms of human life: the seasons of the year, the seasons of the Church, and the seasons of the heart. Within each season recipes are grouped in the order in which they come at the meal, from soup to dessert.

Each recipe is accompanied by a quotation, and many include art that is intended to reflect the nearly two-thousand-year-old experience of monastic life as an affirmation of wholeness, simplicity, and joy. Some quotations are directly about monastic life; others represent the same spirit of affirmation from secular life.

Many monasteries sell locally the food products they make, such as bread, cheese, and jellies. Contemplative monasteries are strung like rosary beads all across North America, as they are also on every continent. You may wish to seek out the one nearest you, not only to inquire whether it sells food, but to experience, in the monastery chapel, the grace and joy that is generated in the twenty-first century centers of contemplative life.

Useful Tips for a Healthier Diet

1. Use herbs and spices as salt substitutes.

2. Use more low-fat and skim milk than regular milk and substitute low-fat yogurt for cream.

3. Many main courses can be served with light rather than rich sauces.

4. Sauté with olive oil or canola oil rather than butter or margarine. Those on low-fat diets may reduce the amounts of oil or margarine or other fats in these recipes by one fourth or more.

5. Eat fresh whole wheat and whole grain breads instead of white bread.

6. Cook with fresh vegetables rather than canned or frozen ones.

7. Be aware of portion sizes and the nutrition content of foods.

8. Serve fruit for dessert.

Winter

"Listen, my son, and with your heart
hear the principles of your Master.
Readily accept and faithfully follow
the advice of a loving Father."

—Prologue to the
Rule of Saint Benedict

Hermit's Soup

Ingredients   *1–2 servings*

1 turnip   3 tablespoons oil of choice
2 carrots   1/3 cup rice
1 small cabbage   2 quarts water
1 onion   salt to taste

1. Wash and trim the vegetables. Slice thinly.

2. Sauté vegetables in oil for a few minutes in a soup pot. Add the rice and water, stir well, cover the pot, and simmer slowly for 1 hour. Add the salt just before serving.

"Solitude, prayer, love, and abstinence are the four wheels of the vehicle that carries our spirit heavenward."

—Saint Seraphim of Sarov

Potato Soup

4 tablespoons butter
1 onion, finely minced
2 quarts milk
4 cups mashed potatoes

2 tablespoons flour
4 tablespoons parsley, chopped
salt and pepper to taste

1. Melt the butter in a skillet and gently sauté the onion, without browning, until soft.

2. Transfer the onion to the top of a double boiler. Add the milk, flour, and potatoes. Stir thoroughly with a wire whip or mixer until smooth. Cover; heat slowly over hot water until soup comes to a boil.

3. Reduce the heat and simmer for 10 minutes. Add salt and pepper to taste; sprinkle with parsley and serve.

"Consider your own call, brothers and sisters: not many of you were wise according to worldly standards, not many were powerful, not many were of noble birth; but God chose what is foolish in the world to shame the wise, God chose what is weak in the world to shame the strong…so that no human being might boast in the presence of God. God is the source of your life."

—1 Corinthians 1:26–30

Saint Nicholas Soup

(Potage Saint-Nicholas)

Ingredients   *6–8 servings*

2 leeks or onions
5 medium carrots
2 turnips
5 potatoes
1/2 head medium cabbage

4 tablespoons butter
1 teaspoon salt (or more, according to taste)
4 quarts water
1/3 cup chervil, minced
croutons

1. Peel and dice the vegetables. Shred the cabbage.

2. Melt the butter in a large soup pot. Add the vegetables, salt, and stir. Turn off the heat, cover the pot, and let it rest for 15 to 20 minutes.

3. Add the water and bring the soup to a boil. Reduce the heat to low to medium, cover the pot, and cook slowly for 30 to 40 minutes. Stir from time to time.

4. When the soup is done, purée in a blender until it is creamy and smooth. Serve hot, garnished with chervil and croutons.

Saint Nicholas, a bishop of Myra in the fourth century, is one of the best-loved saints in both the Eastern and Western churches. He was the original "Santa Claus," and in many countries of Europe presents were exchanged on December 6, his feast day. From Europe the lovely custom of giving gifts during the Christmas season came to America. Because the feast of Saint Nicholas usually falls within the first week of Advent, he is considered an Advent saint who joyfully points toward the coming of the Lord. Today, in some European monasteries, his feast is celebrated with revivals of medieval plays about his life.

Chickpea Soup

Ingredients

2 cups chickpeas
2 cups canned tomatoes
1 large onion, chopped
1 stalk celery, minced
2 carrots, sliced
4 garlic cloves, minced

1 red pepper, diced
4 tablespoons olive oil
1 bouillon cube
1 bay leaf
salt and pepper to taste

1. Soak chickpeas overnight. Cover with water and bring to a boil. Add all remaining ingredients and cook slowly over medium heat for about 1 hour, until the chickpeas and vegetables are tender.

2. Adjust seasoning. Cover and simmer the soup for about 15 minutes. Remove the bay leaf. Serve hot.

"In the midst of winter, I realized that deep within me was an invincible summer."

—Albert Camus

Saint Anthony of the Desert Soup

Ingredients   *4 servings*

3 tablespoons oil of choice
1 cup barley
1 carrot, finely grated
2 leeks, sliced
1 bay leaf

1/3 cup fresh parsley, minced
salt to taste
7 cups water
1 bouillon cube, if desired
chopped mushrooms, if desired

1. Heat the oil in a soup pot and add the barley, stirring continuously for one minute. Immediately add the carrot, leeks, bay leaf, parsley, salt, and water.

2. Cook the soup over low to medium heat, covered, for 40 to 45 minutes, until the barley is tender. Add more water if needed. For extra taste, add the bouillon and the mushrooms during the last 20 minutes of simmering. Remove the bay leaf. Serve hot.

Saint Anthony, called the Great, lived in Egypt between A.D. 251 and 356. At age 18, the gospel text "If you wish to be perfect, go and sell all that you have and then follow me" so moved him that he left everything behind and retired to an inaccessible place in the wilderness where he dedicated his life to God in manual work and continual prayer. In his old age, he imparted wisdom to his disciples and encouraged them to lead a monastic life. Because he was the first Christian to retire to a monastic life, he is considered to be the first monk and also the father of all monks. His feast is celebrated on January 17.

Potage Bonne Femme

Ingredients

4 tablespoons butter
2 carrots, peeled and sliced
2 leeks, white parts only
1 onion, sliced
2 potatoes, peeled and cubed

1 small turnip, cubed
7 cups water
1/2 cup parsley, finely chopped
salt and pepper to taste
1 cup milk (optional)

1. Melt the butter in a soup pot and add the carrots, leeks, and onion. Sauté the vegetables for a few minutes, stirring continuously.

2. Add the potatoes, turnip, water, 1/4 cup parsley, salt, and pepper. Cover the pot and bring the soup to a boil. Lower the heat, and simmer the soup for about 25 to 30 minutes. When the soup is done, if you wish, add the milk.

3. Blend the soup in a blender, until it turns into an even cream. Serve the soup hot and garnish with the rest of the parsley.

A brother who had been visiting with a hermit said, as he was taking his leave: "Forgive me, Father, for hampering you in keeping your rule." The hermit answered: "My rule is to welcome you with hospitality and to send you on your way in peace."

—an early desert father

Red Beans in Wine

(Haricots rouges au vin)

Ingredients   *6 servings*

4 cups dry red beans
6 tablespoons butter
4 onions, sliced

1 tablespoon flour
1 bottle of red wine
salt and pepper to taste

1. Soak the beans overnight. Cook the beans in salted water for about 1½ to 2 hours, until they are tender. Drain.

2. Melt the butter in a saucepan and lightly brown the onions, then remove with a slotted spoon. Add the flour and stir to make a roux. Add the wine slowly, continuing to stir until the mixture is a smooth sauce.

3. Add the beans and onions. Cover and simmer for 30 minutes, stirring from time to time so beans on bottom do not burn. Serve hot with rice, fish, or eggs.

"Our hope is that the winter of humanity will gradually be transformed to the bursting forth of love, for it is to this that we are called."

—Jean Vanier

Leeks au Gratin

(Poireaux au Gratin)

Ingredients   *4–6 servings*

> 12 leeks
> 1 cup grated Gruyère cheese (or similar cheese)
> butter
> salt and pepper

White Sauce
> 4 tablespoons butter
> 4 tablespoons flour
> 2 cups milk

1. Prepare white sauce according to instructions on page 146.

2. Select fresh leeks. Wash and clean them well, trimming the top where the leaves begin to get hard. Cook in boiling salted water for 30 minutes. Rinse and drain them thoroughly.

3. Preheat oven to 350°. Butter an oblong baking dish and cover the entire bottom with 1 cup white sauce. Attractively arrange the leeks in the dish and cover them with the rest of the white sauce. Sprinkle the surface with the grated Gruyère cheese. Bake for 25 to 30 minutes.

Saint Antony the Great said: "When I was visiting an abbot, a virgin came and said to the old man, 'Abba, I spend my life fasting; I eat once a week and study the Old and New Testaments every day.' The old man answered, 'Have poverty and plenty be-come a matter of indifference to you?' 'No,' she said. 'Disgrace and praise?' 'No,' she said. 'Enemies and friends?' 'No,' she said. Then the wise old man said, 'Go and work, you have achieved nothing.'"

—letter from a Russian monk

Stuffed Acorn Squash

Ingredients   *6 servings*

3 medium acorn squashes   1 egg
olive oil   1/3 cup milk
1 large onion, chopped   1 cup bread crumbs
3 garlic cloves, finely minced   salt and pepper to taste
6 tablespoons parsley, minced   grated cheese of your choice
6 mushrooms, finely chopped

1. Wash and rinse the squashes. Cut in half and remove seeds. Fill a large saucepan with water and bring to boil. Place the squashes in the pan, cut side down, and boil for 8 to 10 minutes. Drain immediately.

2. Heat a sufficient amount of oil in a large skillet and sauté the onion, garlic, parsley, and mushrooms for a few minutes, stirring continuously.

3. In a deep bowl, beat the egg and milk together. Add the vegetable mixture and bread crumbs. Mix well and season to taste.

4. Preheat oven to 350°. Butter a flat baking dish and arrange the acorn squash halves in it. Divide the vegetable mixture evenly among the squash halves, filling the cavities. Sprinkle with grated cheese and add 1 teaspoon of oil to the center of each squash half. Bake for 20 to 25 minutes. Serve hot.

"Idleness is an enemy of the soul. Therefore the brethren should be occupied at certain times in manual labor, and at other times in sacred reading. For they are truly monks when they live by the labor of their hands, as did our fathers and the apostles."

—from the Holy Rule of Saint Benedict

Saint Stephen's Scrambled Eggs

(Oeufs brouillés Saint-Étienne)

Ingredients   *6 servings*

6 tomatoes   salt and pepper to taste

3 tablespoons oil   4 tablespoons butter

6 eggs   6 large onions, sliced

6 tablespoons heavy cream

1. Preheat oven to 250°.

2. Choose 6 large, firm tomatoes and slice off the top part of each. Scoop out the insides, being careful to leave the shells intact. Heat the oil in a large skillet and with care cook the tomatoes for 1 or 2 minutes, first with the cut side down so that the water from the tomatoes evaporates. Turn the tomatoes carefully, cook the other side for 1 or 2 minutes. The tomatoes must remain firm. Place the tomato shells in a greased baking dish and keep them warm in the preheated oven.

3. Beat the eggs and cream thoroughly. Add salt and pepper and beat some more. Melt the butter in a large skillet and scramble the eggs. When the eggs are done (there must be some moisture left in them), fill the tomato shells with the eggs and place them back in the oven to keep warm.

4. Pour several tablespoons of oil into the skillet and gently fry the onions until they turn brown. Place the onions in a round serving dish and arrange the 6 tomatoes in the center. Serve hot.

Saint Stephen is considered a Christmas saint because his feast is celebrated the day after Christmas, the 26th of December. Saint Stephen, "a man full of faith and power," was one of the first seven deacons of the early Church, chosen by the apostles to look after the needs of the poor, the orphans, and the widows. He is considered to be the Church's first martyr. While still a young man, he was stoned to death outside the city of Jerusalem for confessing his faith in the Lord Jesus.

Tuna Stuffed Peppers

Ingredients 4 servings

4 green peppers
1 egg, slightly beaten
1/3 cup heavy cream
6 ounces canned tuna fish, flaked
1/2 cup bread crumbs

1 onion, chopped
1/2 cup parsley, chopped and minced
1 tablespoon mustard
salt and pepper to taste
grated cheese of your choice

1. Preheat oven to 350°.

2. Choose large, fresh peppers and boil them whole for about 5 minutes. Drain carefully and allow to cool. Cut the peppers in half and remove the seeds.

3. In a deep bowl, beat the egg and the cream together. Add the remaining ingredients, except the grated cheese, and mix thoroughly.

4. Butter a baking dish and fill the pepper halves with the tuna mixture. Bake for about 20 minutes. Sprinkle the tops with the grated cheese and bake for another 5 minutes, until the cheese melts. Serve hot.

"It is not necessary to fear our weakness.... The most necessary things to fear are devilish pride, vainglory, hostility and condemnation, but weaknesses serve to humble our imagined piety."

—letter from a Russian monk

Lentils and Rice Loaf

(the vegetarian equivalent of meat loaf)

Ingredients

4–6 servings

1 cup lentils
1 cup rice
olive oil
4 cups water
1 large onion, sliced
2 tomatoes, chopped
10 mushrooms, sliced
2 garlic cloves, minced

1 green pepper, diced
3 tablespoons parsley, minced
1 teaspoon thyme
2 eggs
1/3 cup milk
1/2 cup bread crumbs
salt and pepper to taste

1. Preheat oven to 350°. Wash and rinse the lentils. Add the lentils, rice, and 2 tablespoons of oil to the water in a heavy saucepan. Cook over medium heat until they are well done and all water evaporates. (If brown rice is used, you may need more water.)

2. In a large skillet, heat 4 tablespoons oil and gently sauté the onion, tomatoes, mushrooms, garlic, and green pepper until they turn golden. Add the parsley and thyme and stir for 1 or 2 minutes.

3. Beat the eggs in a large bowl. Add the milk, bread crumbs, salt, and pepper and beat some more. Add the lentils, rice, and sautéed vegetables to the egg mixture. Mix everything well; pour into a well-greased bread pan and bake for 40 to 50 minutes. The loaf is done when all liquid has evaporated. Serve hot.

NOTE: You may wish to sauté extra vegetables and serve them as an accompaniment to the loaf.

"See yonder stars so bright and clear
That praise their Maker as they move
And usher in the circling year."

—Schiller

Potato and Parsley Casserole

Ingredients   *6–8 servings*

4 garlic cloves, minced
6 tablespoons oil of choice
8 potatoes, sliced
1 large onion, sliced

1/2 cup parsley, finely chopped
salt and pepper to taste
butter

1. Preheat oven to 350°.

2. Thoroughly butter a 2-quart casserole. Briefly sauté the garlic in the oil; cover the bottom of the casserole dish with it.

3. Fill the casserole with layers as follows: potatoes, onion, parsley, salt, and pepper. Repeat layers. Season and dot top with butter.

4. At the edge of the casserole (so as not to wash off seasonings), add enough water to cover 2/3 to 3/4 of the potatoes. Place a lid on the casserole and bake for about 1 hour, removing the lid for the last 15 minutes.

"Fickleness and indecision are signs of self-love. If you can never make up your mind what God wills for you, but are always veering from one opinion to another…from one method to another, it may be an indication that you are trying to get around God's will and do your own with a quiet conscience. So keep still, and let God do some work."

—Thomas Merton

Subiaco Fish Fillets

1½ cups homemade tomato
   sauce
4 fillets of firm fish
1 egg, slightly beaten
½ cup flour

salt and pepper to taste
2 tablespoons butter
4 tablespoons olive oil
olives, parsley sprigs,
   lemon slices for garnish

1. Prepare a good tomato sauce, following your favorite recipe or the one on page 148, and keep it hot.

2. Dip the fish fillets in egg, then in flour seasoned with salt and pepper.

3. Heat butter and oil in a heavy frying pan and fry the fillets gently for 10 to 15 minutes, depending on their thickness, turning as necessary.

4. Arrange the fillets on a serving platter and place the garnish around them. Spoon some sauce on top of each fillet and serve the rest in a gravy boat.

Mount Subiaco is the holy mountain south of Rome where Saint Benedict retired to live as a hermit at the beginning of his monastic life. At the small monastery still there on the site, the monks joyfully continue to follow in the footsteps of Saint Benedict. The monastery attracts many visitors year-round who come not only to venerate the memory of the patriarch of the West but also to see the beautiful medieval frescoes in the monastic church.

Cabbage and Apples
Béarnaise Style

Ingredients   *6–8 servings*

1 large head cabbage
4 tablespoons sugar
1 teaspoon salt
1/2 cup cider vinegar
4 tablespoons butter, melted

6 tablespoons oil of choice
4 sour apples, peeled and cut into eighths
1/2 cup red wine
2 tablespoons lemon juice

1. Slice the head of cabbage as you would for coleslaw. Place cabbage in a saucepan with the sugar, salt, and cider vinegar. Stir, then cover the pan and let it stand for 30 minutes.

2. Add the butter and oil to the saucepan with the cabbage. Stir thoroughly. Place the apples on the top of the cabbage. Cover the saucepan and cook over low heat, simmering slowly.

3. As the cabbage cooks, add sufficient water to prevent scorching. Cook slowly for 1 hour 20 minutes. Add red wine, lemon juice, and more salt if needed. Heat. The cabbage should be deliciously moist. Serve as an accompaniment to a main course.

"The monk must ever begin again and again, and whatever he does, he remains the unprofitable servant."

—Mother Maria

Corn Meal Mush

(Polenta)

---

1 cup cold water

1 cup yellow corn meal

6 tablespoons oil of choice

1 teaspoon salt

3 cups boiling water

1 cup onion, chopped

2 garlic cloves, crushed

2 green peppers, finely chopped

4 tablespoons olive oil

3/4 teaspoon salt

1 pound canned tomatoes

1 6-ounce can tomato paste

1/2 teaspoon oregano

dash pepper to taste

1 cup yellow cheese, grated

1. Combine cold water, corn meal, oil, and salt. Stir to eliminate lumps. Add mixture to the boiling water, stirring well. Return to boil, stirring constantly. Reduce heat, cover the pot. Cook for 10 minutes, stirring occasionally. Pour into a 10-inch greased ovenproof dish.

2. Sauté onion, garlic, and green peppers in the olive oil. Add salt, tomatoes, tomato paste, oregano, and dash of pepper. Cook, stirring frequently.

3. Reduce heat and simmer for 30 minutes. Preheat oven to 350°. Pour the sauce over the polenta and cover with grated cheese. Bake for 30 minutes, until sauce is bubbly and cheese melts.

"The monks should wait on one another, and let no one be excused from the kitchen service, except by reason of sickness or occupation in some important work. For this service brings increase of reward and of charity."

—from the Holy Rule of Saint Benedict

Leek and Tomato Risotto

Ingredients

4 servings

3 medium-size leeks

3 tomatoes

1/4 cup olive oil

1/2 teaspoon thyme

1/4 teaspoon paprika

1 1/2 cups rice

3 1/2 cups water

salt and pepper to taste

grated Parmesan cheese

1. Preheat oven to 350°.

2. Wash and trim the leeks. Chop the white parts only. Peel and slice the tomatoes.

3. Heat the oil in a good-size ovenproof casserole, add the leeks and tomatoes; simmer for 7 to 8 minutes. Add the thyme, paprika, rice, water, and salt. Stir and bring to a boil.

4. Cover the casserole and bake for 25 to 30 minutes, until all the liquid is absorbed. Check once during the 30 minutes to see if more water is needed. When all the water is absorbed, take the risotto out of the oven, toss it lightly, and serve hot. Sprinkle grated Parmesan cheese over each serving.

"Behave kindly with your neighbors, giving not even the appearance of scorn."

—Saint Seraphim

Saint Syncletica Noodle Casserole

Ingredients   *6–8 servings*

1 pound egg noodles, cooked
2 cups cooked asparagus,
   cut in small pieces
1 large carrot, thinly sliced
1 onion, chopped

1 hard-boiled egg, chopped
1 cup milk
1$\frac{1}{2}$ cups grated Cheddar cheese
salt and pepper to taste
$\frac{1}{2}$ cup bread crumbs

1. Place the cooked noodles, asparagus, carrot, onion, and chopped egg in a deep bowl; mix well.

2. Liberally butter a long, shallow baking dish, and place in it the contents of the bowl. Mix the milk, 1 cup of the grated cheese, salt, and pepper by hand or in a blender, and pour mixture over noodles and vegetables. Toss it lightly and make sure the mixture reaches all corners of the dish.

3. Preheat oven to 300°. Mix the bread crumbs and the remaining $\frac{1}{2}$ cup of cheese together, and sprinkle the mixture over the top of the casserole. Bake in the oven for 30 to 40 minutes, until the top turns brown and bubbly.

Saint Syncletica is one of the earliest desert mothers, and her written life is one of the most ancient documents of monastic hagiography. Some of her spiritual teachings are recorded in the *Sayings of the Desert Fathers*, which gives us a glimpse into the depth of her interior prayer life and wisdom. Her life paralleled that of Saint Antony, the father of monks, and is an inspiration and a model of fidelity to the gospel of Christ.

Mimosa Salad

(Salade mimosa)

Ingredients

2 heads Bibb lettuce
2 heads Boston lettuce

2 Belgium endives
3 hard-boiled eggs, chopped

Tarragon Vinaigrette

8 tablespoons olive oil
2 tablespoons tarragon vinegar
1 tablespoon lemon juice

1 teaspoon French mustard
  (preferably tarragon mustard)
salt and pepper to taste

1. Wash and dry the lettuce and the endives thoroughly. Separate the leaves gently, and place them in a big salad bowl.

2. Just before serving, prepare the vinaigrette according to the directions on page 151. Pour it over the salad and add the hard-boiled eggs. Toss the salad and serve.

"Whatever else be lost among the years,
Let us keep Christmas still a shining thing."

—Grace N. Crowell

SALADS

Broccoli and Tomato Salad

Ingredients   *6 servings*

2 large bunches fresh broccoli   1 bunch arugula, or endives, or mesclun
4 ripe tomatoes

Vinaigrette
8 tablespoons olive oil   1 teaspoon French mustard
2 tablespoons tarragon vinegar   1 shallot, finely minced
2 tablespoons lemon juice   salt and pepper to taste

1. Soak the broccoli in water for one hour. Separate the broccoli florets from the stems. Slice the upper part of the stems thinly and discard the tough parts. Place the broccoli florets and the slices from the stems into a pot of salted boiling water. Boil 5 to 7 minutes. Rinse the broccoli immediately in cold water so that the broccoli maintains its fresh green color.

2. Peel the tomatoes, if desired. Cut them in half and discard the pulp and seeds. Cut the tomatoes in thin slices.

3. Wash and dry the leafy greens and place with broccoli and tomatoes in a salad bowl. Prepare the vinaigrette according to instructions on page 151. Just before serving, pour the vinaigrette over the salad. Toss the salad and serve.

"Except the Christ be born again tonight
In dreams of all men, saints and sons of shame,
The world will never see his kingdom bright."

—Vachel Lindsay

Rainbow Bean Salad

Ingredients   *8 servings*

1 cup green string beans,
   cut small and precooked
1 cup canned red kidney beans
1 cup canned chickpeas
1 cup canned black beans

1 cup canned white beans
   (great northern)
1 cup red onion, finely minced
parsley, finely chopped

Vinaigrette

4 tablespoons olive oil
2 tablespoons lemon juice

$1/2$ tablespoon powdered mustard
salt and freshly ground pepper to taste

1. Cut and precook the green string beans. Using a colander, rinse the canning liquid off the beans by running cold water over them. Drain thoroughly.

2. Place all the beans, onion, and parsley in a deep mixing bowl. Prepare the vinaigrette in a small separate bowl and then add it to the beans. Toss gently and refrigerate for 1 hour before serving.

"To find is to seek Him unceasingly. Here, indeed, to seek is not one thing and to find another. The reward of the search is to go on searching. The soul's desire is fulfilled by the very fact of its remaining unsatisfied, for really to see God is never to have had one's fill of desiring him."

—Saint Gregory of Nyssa

Crêpes Saint-Gwenolé

Ingredients

4 servings (about 12 crêpes)

3 eggs (for more tender crêpes,
    use only the yolks)
1½ cups flour, sifted
1 cup milk
½ cup water
4 tablespoons butter, melted

2 tablespoons orange liqueur
1 tablespoon sugar
2 tablespoons grated orange rind
powdered sugar (superfine,
    not confectioners')

1. Beat the eggs. Gradually stir in flour, then milk, water, and butter. Batter must "rest," covered and in the refrigerator, for at least 2 hours (overnight is fine).

2. Stir in orange liqueur, sugar, and grated orange rind.

3. Select a small frying pan, preferably one with low sides, no more than 7 inches in diameter. Oil or butter it for each crêpe.

4. For each crêpe, pour about 3 tablespoons of batter into warm pan and rotate to spread batter evenly over surface. Batter should be very thick. (Trial and error will determine best heat or necessity of adding a few tablespoons of milk to thin batter slightly, etc.) When one side of crêpe is golden, run spatula around edge of crêpe, then under it, and turn it to brown other side. As each crêpe is done, sprinkle powdered sugar on the surface and fold it in quarters. Stack and cover with waxed paper. Serve the crêpes warm.

"The proof of love is in the works. Where love exists, it does great things. But where it ceases to act, it ceases to exist."

—Saint Gregory the Great

Pumpkin Pear Sauce

Ingredients   *8 servings*

10 pears or apples   1 teaspoon vanilla extract
1 small pumpkin   1 teaspoon cinnamon (optional)
1/2 cup sugar (or more)   nutmeg to taste
2 tablespoons grated orange rind

1. Wash pears or apples, but do not peel. Cut into chunks and remove seeds. Peel the pumpkin and remove the seeds and pith.

2. Place the pears or apples and pumpkin in a heavy pot; add sugar, orange rind, vanilla, cinnamon, nutmeg, and enough water to cover these ingredients. Cover the pot and cook over low heat for an hour, stirring occasionally, until fruits are tender.

3. Put through food grinder, ricer, or blender, and chill. Serve very cold.

"When you pray, shut your eyes for a moment and try to concentrate your spiritual powers. If you get tired, raise your eyes to the icon or the lighted candle. Concentrating on prayer this way, the heart will find within itself that spiritual warmth which comes from Christ himself and fills one's whole being with peace and joy."

—Saint Seraphim of Sarov

Gaudete Date and Rice Pudding

Ingredients   *4 servings*

1 cup rice   1 cup dates, chopped
2 cups water   1/2 cup raisins
1 teaspoon salt   3 tablespoons cognac
1 cup milk   whipping cream
1/3 cup brown sugar   confectioners' sugar
1 egg, well beaten

1. Simmer the rice in salted water in a large saucepan until the rice is done.

2. In a separate saucepan, dissolve the brown sugar in the cup of milk. Add the well-beaten egg, chopped dates, raisins, and 2 tablespoons of cognac; cook over low heat for about 5 minutes, stirring continuously. Simmer for another 5 minutes. Combine this mixture and the rice in a deep bowl and fold together thoroughly. Divide the mixture into 4 dessert dishes and chill for at least 2 hours.

3. Before serving, whip the cream with a mixer, slowly adding confectioners' sugar according to taste and one tablespoon of cognac. Top each dish with a good portion of whipped cream and serve cold.

"For who hath naught to give but love,
   Gives all his heart away,
And giving all, hath all to give,
   Another Christmas Day."

—Charles W. Kennedy

Cloister Molasses-Apple Cake

Ingredients   *6–8 servings*

1$^1/_2$ cups apples, peeled and $^1/_2$ cup sugar
   thinly sliced   1 teaspoon cinnamon
$^3/_4$ cup molasses $^1/_2$ teaspoon cloves
$^1/_3$ cup margarine or shortening $^1/_4$ teaspoon nutmeg
$^1/_2$ cup hot water   1 tablespoon baking powder
2$^1/_2$ cups flour $^1/_4$ teaspoon salt

1. Preheat oven to 350°.

2. Cook the apples in the molasses slowly until they are tender, stirring frequently to prevent scorching.

3. Melt the margarine or shortening in the hot water. Sift all dry ingredients and gradually add to the hot-water mixture, stirring constantly to keep smooth. Stir in molasses and apple mixture.

4. Pour the entire mixture into a well-greased oblong 8-by-12-inch pan. Bake for about 30 minutes. Serve warm.

"The monastery should be so established that all the necessary things, such as water, mill, garden and various workshops may be within the enclosure so that there is no necessity for the monks to go outside of it, since that is not at all profitable for their souls."

—from the Holy Rule of Saint Benedict

Apple Compote

2 cups water
1/2 cup sugar (depending
    on sweetness of apples)
2 pounds apples (peeled, cored,
    and cut in halves or quarters
    depending on size)

2 pieces lemon peel
5 whole cloves

1. Heat water and sugar together. When sugar is completely dissolved, add apples, lemon peel, and cloves. Cook about 20 minutes over high heat.

2. Chill and serve.

"I have come to the conclusion that the most important element in human life is faith. If God were to take away all the blessings, health, physical fitness, wealth, intelligence, and leave me with but one gift, I would ask for faith—for with faith in God, in God's goodness, mercy, love for me, and belief in everlasting life, I believe I could still be happy, trustful, leaving all to God's inscrutable providence."

—Rose Kennedy

Twelfth Night Cake

Ingredients   *6–8 servings*

1 cup shortening
2²/₃ cups sugar
5¹/₂ cups flour
5 teaspoons baking powder

¹/₂ teaspoon salt
1¹/₂ cups milk
6 egg whites, stiffly beaten
2 teaspoons vanilla extract

Icing

2 cups confectioners' sugar
¹/₂ cup butter or margarine

2 tablespoons milk or cream
gumdrops

1. Preheat oven to 375°.

2. Cream shortening and sugar until fluffy. Sift dry ingredients together. Add milk alternately with the sifted dry ingredients to the creamed mixture.

3. Fold in beaten egg whites. Add vanilla and stir.

4. Divide batter evenly between three 9-inch greased layer cake pans and bake for about 30 minutes.

5. Prepare the icing by beating the ingredients (except gumdrops) together until stiff. Spread icing between layers and on top as a frosting. Decorate the top with a crown of gumdrops.

"Happy, happy Christmas, that can take us back to the delusions of our childish days, that can recall to the old man the pleasures of his youth and transport the traveler, thousands of miles away, back to his own friends and his quiet home."

—Charles Dickens

Dutchess County Apple and Pear Tart

Ingredients

8 servings

3 cooking apples, thinly sliced
3 cooking pears, thinly sliced
6 tablespoons apple brandy
2 tablespoons lemon juice

$^1/_4$ teaspoon nutmeg
4 ounces apple jelly
2 egg whites, stiffly beaten

Pastry Shell

2 cups flour
1 stick butter or margarine
pinch of salt

2 egg yolks
5 tablespoons ice water

1. Prepare the pastry shell according to directions on page 155. Prebake at 350° for about 12 minutes.

2. Mix the fruit slices with the brandy, lemon juice, and nutmeg.

3. Fill the pastry shell with an even apple and pear layer, following the design of a revolving wheel. Cover the surface with half the apple jelly. Place another layer of fruit on top of the first one. Cover with the remaining apple jelly and top with the beaten egg whites. Bake at 350° for about 30 to 40 minutes. Let cool before serving.

NOTE: Dutchess County in New York State, home of Our Lady of the Resurrection, is rich agricultural land, well known for the marvelous apples and pears it produces. The long rows of apple orchards across the county enhance the beauty of the rural landscape. Unfortunately, the pressure of development on local farmers is such that unless local officials protect the county's long tradition of agriculture, farms and orchards may soon be a thing of the past.

"Blessed by the LORD be his land, with the choice gifts of heaven above, and of the deep that lies beneath; with the choice fruits of the sun, and the rich yield of the months...."

—Deuteronomy 33:13–14

Christmas Day Bread

(Christstollen)

Ingredients   *2 large stollens*

1 package or cake of yeast
1 tablespoon sugar
1/4 cup lukewarm water
1 cup shortening
1 1/4 cups sugar
2 eggs
2 cups milk, scalded
6 cups flour

1 teaspoon salt
1/2 teaspoon nutmeg
1 cup raisins
1 cup currants
1/2 cup blanched almonds
1/2 cup citron, chopped
1 1/2 teaspoons lemon extract

1. Dissolve yeast and 1 tablespoon sugar in warm water. Cover and allow to bubble up. Cream shortening and sugar in large bowl. Sift together flour, salt, and nutmeg.

2. Cool milk to lukewarm and mix with eggs. Add liquid alternately with flour to the creamed mixture. Stir in yeast mixture. Add fruits and flavoring. Knead until smooth. Cover and let dough rise to double its bulk.

3. Preheat oven to 400°. Knead dough again. Shape into ropes about 1 1/2 inches in diameter. For each large stollen, make one rope 3 feet long and two that are 2 1/2 feet long. Braid the ropes together, shaping the braid to a point at either end.

4. Place the braid on a greased cookie sheet. Bake for 25 minutes or until golden.

"As fits the holy Christmas birth.
    Be this, good friend, our carols still—
Be peace on earth, be peace on earth,
    To men of gentle will."

—William M. Thackeray

Epiphany Bread

Ingredients   *5 loaves (cakelike)*

4 cups milk, scalded
3 1/2 cups sugar
3 1/2 teaspoons salt
11 eggs
1 cup butter, melted

7 packages yeast
  (dissolved in 1 1/3 cups warm water)
2 1/2 pounds raisins
  (soak in 1/4 to 1/2 cup warm water)
16 to 17 cups flour

1. In a large, heavy pan, scald the milk. Add sugar and salt. Cool. Beat eggs and add with melted butter and dissolved yeast to the cooled milk mixture. Add raisins, including the extra water.

2. Measure 14 cups flour into a large bowl and beat in the above mixture. Add additional flour as needed, but the batter should be a little sticky. Cover and let rise to double in size, then punch down.

3. Form into loaves and place in greased loaf pans. Let rise in pans until double in size. Bake in a preheated 325° oven for about 50 minutes.

"We shall not cease from exploration
And the end of all our exploring
Will be to arrive where we started
And know the place for the first time."

—T. S. Eliot

Whole Wheat Buttermilk Bread

(a quick bread from South Africa)

Ingredients   *1 loaf*

1 cup white flour
2 heaping cups coarsely ground
   whole wheat flour
3 tablespoons sesame seeds
2 tablespoons toasted wheat germ

1 tablespoon brown sugar or honey
1 teaspoon salt
1 heaping teaspoon baking soda
2 cups buttermilk

1. Preheat oven to 400°.

2. Mix all the dry ingredients thoroughly. Make a well in the center and add all of the buttermilk at once. Combine ingredients and add a little water if the mixture is too dry.

3. Grease and flour a bread pan. Pour the mixture into the pan and bake for about 40 minutes. Cool and serve.

"Friendship is a basket of bread from which to eat for years to come. Good loaves fragrant and warm miraculously multiplied; the basket never empty and the bread never stale."

—Catherine de Vinck

Spring

"Let us encompass ourselves with faith and the practice of good works, and guided by the Gospel, tread the path He has cleared for us. Thus may we deserve to see Him, Who has called us into His Kingdom."

—Prologue to the Rule of Saint Benedict

Minestrone Monastico

Ingredients   *6–8 servings*

3 quarts water

4 carrots

1 cup dry white beans

4 potatoes

1 cup green beans

2 celery stalks

3 onions

1/2 cup plus 2 tablespoons olive oil

1 cup white wine

1 cup macaroni

tarragon, minced

salt and pepper to taste

grated Parmesan cheese

1. Wash the vegetables and peel the carrots, potatoes, and onions. Cut all vegetables in small pieces. Pour the water into a large pot and add all the vegetables, except the onions. Cook slowly over medium heat for 1 hour.

2. Sauté the onions in the 2 tablespoons of oil in a large frying pan until golden. Reserve.

3. After an hour of slow cooking, add the onions, wine, olive oil to taste (up to 1/2 cup), macaroni, tarragon, salt, and pepper. Continue cooking for another 15 minutes. Cover the pan and allow soup to simmer for 10 minutes. Serve the minestrone hot, with grated Parmesan cheese.

"At appointed times monks ought to be occupied with holy reading. Each monk shall receive a book from the library, which he should read from cover to cover. These books should be handed out at the beginning of Lent."

—from the Holy Rule of Saint Benedict

Cream of Asparagus Soup

$1/2$ pound fresh asparagus,
   cut in 1-inch pieces
1 potato, diced
1 onion, diced
1 medium carrot, sliced

2 quarts water
1 cup half-and-half
2 tablespoons butter
salt and pepper to taste

1. Cook the vegetables in the salted water until they are tender. Put the soup through a sieve, food mill, or blender.

2. Return the soup to the saucepan, add the half-and-half, butter, salt, and pepper. Stir and bring almost to a boil. Stir again, cover the pan, and simmer for 10 minutes. Serve hot.

NOTE: For a soup of thicker consistency, substitute 1 cup of white sauce for the cream.

"Even if monks live in the desert, far from the tumult of the city and public affairs, they neglect nothing either in their actions or in their words, to make of their heart an inviolable sanctuary and to preserve intact that purity which permits them to enter into communication with God to the degree compatible with human strength."

—Saint John Chrysostom

Vermicelli Soup

(Potage au vermicelli)

Ingredients   *6 servings*

2 1/2 quarts water
3 garlic cloves, minced
1 onion, minced
2 carrots, cut in small cubes

6 vegetable bouillon cubes
3 ounces vermicelli noodles
1/2 cup fresh parsley, minced
salt to taste

1. Bring the water to a boil in a large soup kettle. Add the bouillon and vegetables, except parsley, and cook for about 20 minutes. Add the vermicelli noodles and continue cooking for another 10 minutes over medium heat.

2. When the vegetables are tender, add the parsley and salt. Cover the kettle and simmer for 10 more minutes. Serve hot.

NOTE: The flavor of this easy soup is greatly enhanced when homemade bouillon is used. White wine may also be added to the broth.

"This is the value of the Resurrection—that things unvalued now reveal their worth."

—Lucy Larcom

Asparagus Stuffed Eggs

Ingredients   *4 servings*

8 eggs, hard-boiled   mayonnaise
2 tablespoons parsley, minced   salt and pepper to taste
1 cup asparagus tips, cooked   tomatoes (optional)
1 tablespoon French mustard   olives (optional)

1. Cut the hard-boiled eggs in half lengthwise. Gently remove the yolks and place them in a bowl. Add the cooked asparagus and parsley and thoroughly mash everything together, or process in a blender until smooth.

2. Add mustard, enough mayonnaise for moisture, salt, and pepper, and blend well. Fill the egg white halves with the mixture and serve with slices of ripe tomato and olives.

"In a pleasant spring morning all sins are forgiven. Such a day is a truce to give. While such a sun holds out to burn, the vilest sinner may return. Through our own recovered innocence we discern the innocence of our neighbors."

—Henry David Thoreau

Scalloped Parsnips

Ingredients   *6 servings*

10 parsnips
1 onion, thinly sliced
1/3 cup fresh parsley, chopped
2 cups tomato sauce
  (preferably homemade)

1/2 cup bread crumbs
1/2 cup grated cheese of your choice
salt and pepper to taste (optional)

1. Wash and clean the parsnips. Slice, then boil them for 15 minutes. Drain off the liquid and stir in the onion, parsley, and tomato sauce.

2. Preheat oven to 375°. Grease a flat baking dish and spread the parsnip-tomato sauce mixture evenly. Add salt and pepper if you wish. Cover with bread crumbs and the grated cheese. Bake for 35 to 40 minutes. Serve hot.

"For there is hope of a tree, if it be
cut down, that it will sprout again,
and that the tender branch thereof
will not cease."

—Job 14:7

Saint Mary of Egypt Fava Beans

(Fèves Sainte-Marie l'Egyptienne)

Ingredients   *4–6 servings*

12 ounces fava beans   1/4 cup sesame oil
2 leeks, sliced   parsley
2 onions, sliced   salt
2 garlic cloves, minced

1. Soak the beans overnight. Rinse and boil them for about 30 minutes in fresh water, until they are tender. Drain.

2. Sauté the leeks, onions, and garlic in sesame oil in a large skillet, stirring from time to time until the onions begin to turn golden. Add the cooked beans, 1/3 cup water, salt, and parsley. Continue cooking for 15 minutes over low to medium heat with pan covered. Stir occasionally so that the vegetables do not burn on the bottom, and add water if necessary.

3. Turn down the heat and simmer for an additional 10 to 15 minutes. Serve hot.

Saint Mary of Egypt is one of those desert saints who has a timeless appeal to all those who seek God by way of the monastic life. Mary was a fifth-century harlot from Alexandria who, after praying before the icon of the Mother of God in a church in Jerusalem, was somehow mysteriously touched by God's grace. After her conversion, she crossed the river Jordan to live an austere life of prayer and penance. Her feast is celebrated on April 2.

Candied Sweet Potatoes with Raisins

Ingredients   *6–8 servings*

4 tablespoons butter

8 sweet potatoes

1 cup raisins

1 cup brown sugar

1 cup sweet wine

1 cup water

$1/2$ teaspoon salt

1. Peel the potatoes and cut them lengthwise in $1/2$-inch thick slices.

2. Preheat the oven to 300°. Melt the butter in a large skillet. Add the potatoes, raisins, and sugar. Stir for 1 or 2 minutes, until the potatoes are evenly coated.

3. Butter a flat baking dish and arrange the potatoes attractively in it. Mix together all the remaining ingredients. Cover the dish and bake for about 45 minutes. Uncover and continue baking for another 20 minutes. Serve hot.

"If you wish to put in order the inner dwelling-place of your soul, prepare the material necessary so that the heavenly architect can begin his work. In order for the dwelling to be light, so that the light of heaven can come in, there must be windows, which are our five senses. The door of the abode is Christ…who guards both the dwelling and its inhabitants."

—Saint Seraphim of Sarov

Crêpes with Camembert Cheese

(Crêpes au Camembert)

Ingredients   *12 crepes*

1 cup flour
2 eggs
1½ cups milk
4 tablespoons vegetable or canola oil

salt to taste
8 ounces Camembert cheese
4 teaspoons chives, finely chopped
(optional)

1. Place the flour in a mixing bowl and form a hollow in the center. Add the eggs and beat with an electric mixer. Gradually add the milk and beat until the batter is thoroughly smooth and of a thick, light consistency. Beat in the oil and salt.

2. Slice the cheese into small pieces and crumble. Add to the batter. Mix well.

3. Oil or butter a 7-inch crêpe pan. For each crêpe, use about 7 tablespoons of the batter (as much as necessary to cover the bottom of the pan) and swirl around. Cook one side briefly until it turns light brown, and then, with the help of a spatula, turn and cook the other side. Roll the crêpes and serve them while still warm.

"Let the oratory be what it is called, a place of prayer, and let nothing else be done there. Let reverence for God be preserved there."

—from the Holy Rule of Saint Benedict

Acorn Squash Stuffed with Cottage Cheese

Ingredients   *4 servings*

2 medium acorn squashes
8 ounces cottage cheese
1/3 cup chives, finely chopped

1/3 cup chervil or parsley, chopped
salt to taste

1. Cut squash in half and hollow out the insides. Fill a large saucepan with water and bring to boil. Place the squash halves cut side down in the water and boil them for about 15 minutes, until they are cooked but still firm.

2. While the squash is cooking, thoroughly combine the cottage cheese, chives, and chervil or parsley. Drain the squash halves and fill with the cottage cheese and herb mixture. Serve immediately.

NOTE: An easy and nutritious dish or a light lunch.

"It all adds up to one thing: peace, silence, solitude. The world and its noise are out of sight and far away. Forest and fields, sun and wind and sky, earth and water, all speak the same silent language."

—Thomas Merton

Asparagus Saint Cassian

2 pounds asparagus

6 sprigs Italian parsley, chopped

6 mint leaves

6 sprigs chervil, chopped

small bunch of fresh chives, chopped

4 tablespoons low-fat plain yogurt

2 tablespoons fresh lemon juice

2 tablespoons olive oil

salt and freshly ground pepper to taste

1. Cook the asparagus standing, tips up, in about 3 inches of water. Cover the pot and let them steam for about 7 minutes. Drain the asparagus and place it on a large platter.

2. Prepare a sauce by combing all the remaining ingredients in a blender. Blend thoroughly. Taste and check the seasonings. Pour the sauce over the asparagus and serve immediately.

Saint John Cassian is one of the most eloquent interpreters of the early monastic movement that originated in the deserts of Egypt and Palestine. After he was ordained a deacon by Saint John Chrysostom in Constantinople, he sojourned for several years in the desert, where monasticism was flourishing at the time. Drawing on his own monastic experience, he then journeyed to the West, and settled in Marseilles. In France, he transmitted the monastic tradition in all its original purity to the people until his death in A.D. 433.

Linguine with Broccoli and Tofu

Ingredients

1/2 pound linguine
1/2 pound tofu
3 cups broccoli spears (florets)
8 garlic cloves, minced

1/2 cup olive oil
1/2 cup grated cheese of your choice
salt and pepper to taste

1. Cook linguine in a large pot of salted water for about 8 to 9 minutes, until tender.

2. Wash, rinse, and cut the tofu in small cubes. Steam the tofu with the broccoli for about 5 to 7 minutes in a small amount of water.

3. Brown the garlic in the olive oil, stirring continuously for a minute or two.

4. Drain the linguine, broccoli, and tofu, and place them in a large serving bowl. Add the salt and pepper and pour the garlic sauce over the mixture. Mix well, sprinkle with grated cheese, and serve while it is steaming hot.

"I believe that it is the witness of the monk to the eternal, to preach the tenderness of God, and to live it."

—Mother Maria

Vegetable-Noodle Casserole

12 ounces broad egg noodles
2 cups eggplant, diced
2 medium tomatoes, sliced
1 green pepper, chopped
1 onion, chopped

1 tablespoon parsley, chopped
garlic powder
salt and pepper
1 cup grated yellow American cheese
Parmesan cheese

1. Preheat oven to 350°.

2. Cook noodles according to package directions and drain.

3. Sauté vegetables and seasonings gently in oil until softened. Combine noodles, vegetable mixture, and cheese in a buttered casserole dish. Sprinkle top with Parmesan cheese. Bake for about 30 minutes.

"This rule in gardening never forget,
To sow dry and set wet."

—old proverb

Festive Lasagna

Ingredients   *6–8 servings*

1 pound lasagna noodles
olive oil
3/4 pound ricotta or cottage cheese

1 pound mozzarella cheese
wheat germ

Tomato Sauce

1 large onion, chopped
1 carrot, thinly sliced
3 garlic cloves, minced
olive oil
12 ounces tomato purée

7 cups canned tomatoes, strained
bay leaf
1/4 cup basil, minced
2 pinches oregano
salt and pepper to taste

1. To make sauce, lightly sauté onion, carrot, and garlic in oil. Stir in tomato purée and strained whole tomatoes. Add bay leaf, basil, and oregano. Simmer about 2 hours, stirring to prevent burning, until sauce is of desired thickness. Add salt sparingly at the last minute. Add pepper if a spicier sauce is desired.

2. Preheat oven to 375°. Cook noodles according to package directions. Oil the bottom of a large baking dish and arrange the ingredients in liberal layers as follows: sauce, noodles, sauce, noodles, ricotta (cottage cheese), noodles, sauce. Top with sliced mozzarella cheese, sauce, and sprinkle surface with wheat germ. Bake for about 30 minutes.

"The story of Easter is the story of God's wonderful window of divine surprise."

—Carl Knudsen

French-Style Fish Fillets with Herbs

(Filets aux herbes)

Ingredients 6 servings

1 pound firm fish fillets
½ cup dry white wine or
   dry vermouth
½ cup water

salt and pepper to taste
1 onion, chopped
parsley, chives, chervil, thyme
2 tablespoons butter

1. Preheat oven to 350°.

2. Arrange the fish fillets in an oven-to-table baking dish.

3. Combine the wine or vermouth, water, seasonings, onion, and herbs, and pour over the fish. Dot with butter. Bake 30 minutes, basting from time to time. Serve from the baking dish, spooning the juices over each portion.

"I believe that without the impetus of love, it is not possible to begin or continue any journey of the spirit. But love, too, must know its measure and its limitations."

—Sister Thekla

Cheese Soufflé

1 cup grated Parmesan or
  Romano cheese
3 tablespoons margarine or butter
3 tablespoons white flour
  or cornstarch

1 cup milk
salt, pepper, nutmeg to taste
1/2 pound grated sharp Cheddar cheese
6 eggs, separated

1. Preheat oven to 375°.

2. Generously butter a 2-quart soufflé dish and coat the bottom and sides with the Parmesan or Romano cheese, using the entire cup.

3. Prepare cheese sauce: melt margarine or butter, add flour or cornstarch, and stir until smooth. Add milk slowly, stirring and cooking over low to medium heat until thickened. Stir in seasonings and Cheddar cheese gradually, beating until smooth. (If too thick, add more milk.)

4. Add beaten egg yolks to cheese sauce. Cool sauce. Beat egg whites until very stiff and fold into cooled cheese-yolk mixture—don't beat.

5. Pour mixture into soufflé dish. Bake 30 minutes without opening oven until lightly brown. Serve immediately.

NOTE: For a spinach soufflé, add chopped cooked spinach, well drained (1 pound fresh or frozen), and 1 chopped onion, sautéed, to cheese-yolk mixture.

"But unless humility, simplicity, and goodness adorn our lives, and are associated with prayer, the mere formality of prayer will avail us nothing. And this I say, not of prayer only, but of every other outward exercise or labor undertaken with a notion of virtue."

—Saint Macarius

Fennel Gratin Saint Colette

Ingredients *6 servings*

fennel bulbs   grated Parmesan cheese
salt to taste   butter

1. Trim the fennel bulbs and cut them in half lengthwise. Place them carefully in a double boiler, and sprinkle some salt on top. Cover the pot and cook for 15 minutes.

2. Preheat the oven to 350°. Butter a baking dish and carefully place (so that they remain intact) the fennel bulbs in the dish. Sprinkle grated cheese on top of each bulb and add a small dot of butter in each center.

3. Bake the fennel for 10 to 15 minutes, until the tops turn brown. Serve hot. This is a delicious appetizer to an elegant dinner. It can also be served as a side dish.

"The life of the soul is truth and the awareness of the soul is love."

—Saint Bernard

Artichokes Peasant Style

Ingredients

6 servings

6 artichokes, small (baby kind)
1 onion, sliced
1 carrot, thinly sliced
3 tomatoes, peeled and
   sliced in quarters

1/2 cup olive oil
11/2 cups dry white wine
1 bay leaf
6 parsley sprigs, chopped
salt and pepper to taste

1. Sauté the artichokes, onion, carrot, and tomatoes in olive oil for several minutes, stirring frequently.

2. Add the white wine, bay leaf, parsley, salt, and pepper. Stir, then cover the pot. Simmer slowly, until artichokes are soft and tender. Remove the bay leaf. Serve hot.

"The monk works with his hands not only to earn his living, but above all for the good of his soul."

—Saint Jerome

Poached Eggs à la Charentaise

Ingredients *6 servings*

6 medium-size potatoes, peeled
6 tablespoons butter or margarine
salt, pepper, nutmeg to taste
$1/2$ cup grated Gruyère cheese
   (or substitute with Parmesan)

6 eggs
1 pint heavy cream
finely chopped chives as garnish

1. Slice the potatoes into thin slices and sauté in melted butter until they are cooked and slightly browned on both sides. Season with salt, pepper, and a dash of nutmeg. Stir often.

2. Thoroughly butter an elongated baking dish and sprinkle it with the grated cheese. Evenly spread the cooked potatoes over the surface of the dish. Sprinkle with more cheese and spread a second layer of potatoes. Sprinkle more grated cheese evenly over the potatoes.

3. Preheat oven to 350°. Break the eggs and place them carefully on the top of the cheese, leaving space in between them. Sprinkle salt and pepper on top of the eggs, according to taste, and evenly cover the dish with the heavy cream.

4. Bake for 12 to 15 minutes, until the eggs are properly cooked. Sprinkle chives on top as a garnish. Serve immediately.

"Every believer in this world of ours must be a spark of light, a center of love, a vivifying leaven amidst his fellow men."

—Pope John XXIII

Braised Radishes and Peas

Ingredients   *4 servings*

4 tablespoons butter or margarine
1 small onion, chopped and minced
2 cups fresh or frozen peas
2 cups radishes (whole)
1½ cups water

1 bouillon cube (vegetable)
½ teaspoon ground marjoram
salt to taste
finely chopped chervil as garnish

1. Melt the butter in a casserole. Add the onion, radishes, and peas. Cook for 4 to 5 minutes, stirring frequently.

2. Add the water, bouillon cube, marjoram, and salt, and stir thoroughly. Cover the casserole and simmer gently for about 15 minutes, or until all the water is absorbed. Serve hot as a side vegetable; garnish with the chervil.

"If we had a keen vision and feeling of all ordinary human life, it would be like hearing the grass grow and the squirrel's heart beat and we should die of that roar which lies on the other side of silence."

—George Eliot

Mixed Salad for Spring

$1\frac{1}{2}$ cups fresh green peas
$1\frac{1}{2}$ cups green beans,
    cut in 1-inch pieces
1 small onion, minced
1 large green pepper, sliced

oil and vinegar dressing
parsley
salt and pepper
3 to 4 tomatoes
3 eggs, hard-boiled

1. Cook peas and green beans. Drain and rinse briefly in cold water. Toss still-warm peas and beans with onion, dressing, seasonings, parsley, and green pepper. Chill.

2. Serve either on a platter surrounded with rings of sliced tomatoes and sliced eggs or stuff salad into hollowed-out tomatoes and surround with egg slices. Good with mayonnaise.

SALADS

"Courage is an inner resolution to go forward despite obstacles; cowardice is submissive surrender to circumstances. Courage breeds creative self-affirmation; cowardice produces destructive self-abnegation. Courage faces fear and masters it; cowardice represses fear and is mastered by it."

—Martin Luther King, Jr.

Raw Spinach-Mushroom Salad

Ingredients   *6–8 servings*

1 pound raw spinach,
    trimmed and torn in bite-size pieces
1 pound mushrooms, sliced

1 red apple, peeled and sliced
1 small onion, thinly sliced
2 eggs, hard-boiled and chopped

Dressing

6 tablespoons oil
2 tablespoons vinegar
1/2 teaspoon salt

1/2 teaspoon pepper
dash of tamari or soy sauce

1. Mix and toss together the spinach, mushrooms, apple, onion, and chopped eggs.

2. Prepare a salad dressing by mixing the oil, vinegar, soy sauce, salt, and pepper. Mix well and pour over the salad. Toss lightly and serve.

NOTE: Nonvegetarians can sprinkle crisp bacon bits on salad.

"The yoke of Christ is sweet and his burden light unto refreshment for those who submit to it; but all things alien to the teachings of the Gospel are heavy and burdensome."

—from the Short Rules of Saint Basil

Rice Salad

(Riz en salade)

Ingredients   *4 servings*

1 cup rice   olive oil
2 cups water   lemon juice
1/2 cup pitted green olives, chopped   salt and pepper to taste
1/2 cup pitted black olives, chopped   1/3 cup parsley, finely chopped

1. Place the rice in a saucepan with 1 tablespoon oil, salt, and pepper, and stir well. Add water, cover tightly, and bring to a rapid boil. Lower the heat and cook the rice slowly for about 20 minutes, until all of the water is absorbed.

2. When the rice is tender, allow it to cool in the refrigerator for at least an hour.

3. Mix the rice and the olives in a large bowl. Add olive oil, lemon juice, salt, and pepper; mix well. Sprinkle the parsley on top and serve the salad cold.

NOTE: This delightful salad can be served on a large platter with cherry tomatoes and slices of hard-boiled eggs.

"God can bring summer out of winter, though we have no spring. All occasions invite his mercies, and all times are his seasons."

—John Donne

Mediterranean Lentil Salad

Ingredients   *6 servings*

2 cups cooked lentils (drained)   5 ounces marinated artichokes, chopped
1 onion, finely chopped   4 ounces pimientos, chopped
5 ounces pitted black olives, chopped

Vinaigrette
2/3 cup olive oil   1 tablespoon mustard
1/4 cup wine vinegar   salt and pepper to taste

1. Place all of the salad ingredients in a large bowl and refrigerate for at least 1 hour.

2. Just before serving, prepare the vinaigrette according to the directions on page 151 and pour over the salad. Mix well and serve cold.

"Let all be silent at the table. No whispering or noise is to be heard, only the voice of the reader. The monks shall pass to one another the food and drink as they have need of it, so that no one may ask for anything. If something is missing, then let it be asked for with a signal rather than verbally."

—from the Holy Rule of Saint Benedict

Saint Seraphim's Cake

Ingredients   *8 servings*

4 ounces sweet butter or margarine   2 teaspoons baking powder
1 cup sugar $1/2$ teaspoon baking soda
2 eggs   1 cup milk
$3/4$ cup cocoa   1 teaspoon vanilla
$1/2$ teaspoon salt $1/3$ cup rum
2 cups unsifted flour

1. Preheat oven to 350°.

2. Cream the butter or margarine and sugar together. Add the eggs, one at a time, beating thoroughly. Add the cocoa and beat another minute.

3. Sift the flour, salt, baking powder, and baking soda into a deep bowl. Combine the milk, vanilla, and rum. Add the dry ingredients slowly to the chocolate mixture, alternating with the wet ingredients. Blend well until totally smooth.

4. Grease and flour a 13-by-9-inch cake pan. Pour the cake mixture into it and bake for 40 to 45 minutes. Check by inserting a toothpick or long pin to see if cake is sufficiently baked. Allow the cake to cool in the pan.

Saint Seraphim is a Russian saint from the eighteenth century who was twenty years old when he entered the monastery at Sarov. His life was similar to that of the desert fathers of fourth-century Egypt. He lived alone in a forest hermitage, where he cultivated a small garden, studied Scripture and the writings of the monastic fathers, and devoted himself to continual prayer. After his health began to fail, he continued his life of seclusion in a small cell in the monastery. A saint of remarkable spiritual insights and prophetic gifts, he was observed *in extasis*, his facial transfiguration producing a "blinding light."

Benedictine Rhubarb and Raisin Pudding

Ingredients   *8 servings*

8 slices whole wheat bread, cubed
1½ cups milk
4 tablespoons butter, melted
4 eggs
1 cup sugar, honey, or molasses,
   depending on taste

1 cup rhubarb, sliced and cooked
1 cup raisins
pinch of salt, nutmeg, and cinnamon

1. Preheat oven to 350°.

2. Place the cubed bread in a mixing bowl. Mix the butter and the milk and pour over bread. Let stand for at least 20 minutes.

3. Beat the eggs in a deep bowl; add the remaining ingredients and mix well. Combine the egg mixture with the bread and milk mixture.

4. Butter a flat baking dish and pour the mixture into it. Bake for about 45 minutes. Serve warm or cold.

"The only justification for the monastic life lies simply in the fact that God calls some people to it. For the monk himself there is no problem. He comes to undertake his life of prayer and work and discipline in the community simply because he knows that that is what God wants him to do. He can, therefore, not do anything else."

—Sister Thekla

Monastery Whole Wheat Bread

Ingredients

3 loaves

3/4 cup honey

1/4 cup molasses

3 cups boiling water

1 cup cold water

3 packages dry yeast

1/4 cup oil of choice

10 cups whole wheat flour

1 teaspoon salt

1. Place honey and molasses in large bowl. Stir in hot water, then add cold water. When liquid is lukewarm, sprinkle yeast evenly over mixture to activate. Add oil and gradually stir in flour and salt.

2. Knead on a well-floured bread board until mixture is even. Place in greased bowl and cover with damp towel. Set in warm place to rise for 1 hour.

3. Punch down and knead. Let rise again for 45 minutes. Knead. Shape and place in well-greased loaf pans. Let rise for 30 minutes. Preheat oven to 350°. Bake for about 30 minutes.

"The bread which you do not use is the bread of the hungry; the garment hanging in your wardrobe is the garment of the one who is naked; the shoes you do not wear are the shoes of the one who is barefoot; the money that you keep locked away is the money of the poor; the acts of charity that you do not perform are so many injustices that you commit."

—Saint Basil the Great

Easter Bread

Ingredients   *2 ring-shaped loaves*

2 cups milk, scalded   1½ teaspoons salt
1 package yeast   ½ cup raisins
6 cups flour   ½ cup candied fruit peel
5 tablespoons shortening   1 teaspoon nutmeg
1 cup sugar   1 egg, slightly beaten
2 eggs, well beaten

1. Cool milk to lukewarm and dissolve yeast in it. Add 2 cups flour and beat well.

2. Cream shortening with sugar; add eggs and beat well. Add milk mixture with salt and remaining flour. Knead well; let rise in a warm place for about 1½ hours. Work in remaining ingredients except for egg, and knead on floured board until dough does not stick.

3. Place in a greased bowl, rub with butter, cover, and let rise until double in bulk. Knead again and shape into 2 rings on a cookie sheet. Brush lightly with the beaten egg and let rise until double again. Preheat oven to 400° and bake for 15 minutes, then reduce heat to 350° and bake for 15 minutes more.

May Easter Day
To thy heart say,
    "Christ died and rose for thee."
May Easter night
On thy heart write,
    "O Christ, I live for thee."

—Anonymous

Paschal Spice Ring

Ingredients

3 tablespoons shortening
1 cup sugar
1 teaspoon baking soda
10 3/4 ounces condensed tomato soup
2 cups flour

1 teaspoon cinnamon
1 teaspoon each mace, nutmeg,
  and cloves, mixed
1 1/2 cups raisins or candied fruit peel

Orange Icing

4 tablespoons soft margarine or butter
1/4 teaspoon salt
1/2 pound confectioners' sugar

1/4 cup frozen orange juice
  concentrate, thawed

1. Preheat oven to 325°.

2. Cream shortening and sugar. Stir baking soda into soup. Sift flour and spices together and combine with the creamed shortening and sugar. Stir well. Add the soup and raisins or candied fruit peel. Mix well. Bake in a 10-inch tube pan for 35 minutes. Remove from pan and allow to cool.

3. To make icing: cream margarine or butter, add salt and a little sugar, and work together well. Add additional sugar and orange juice concentrate alternately in small portions, mixing thoroughly until icing is of good spreading consistency.

4. Frost cake, and when icing has set, place a candle in the hole in the center. (Dripping melted wax at the base will help it stand securely.)

"For I remember it is Easter morn,
And life and love and peace are all new born."

—Alice Palmer

Pentecost Cream

4 eggs
1/2 to 3/4 cup sugar
1/2 cup butter
1 quart milk
1/2 cup flour
peel of 1/2 lemon, sliced in thin strips
1/2 teaspoon anise
1/4 teaspoon nutmeg

1 teaspoon vanilla
1 package (10–12) anisette
    spongecake fingers
2 cups peaches, sliced
1/2 pint whipping cream
1/2 teaspoon brandy
1/2 cup confectioners' sugar
small pinch nutmeg

1. Cream together eggs and sugar.

2. In a saucepan, melt butter. Blend flour with 1 cup of milk, then add remaining milk and lemon peel to saucepan. Cook, stirring continuously, until it starts to thicken, but do not boil. Stir in the sugar-egg mixture, spices, and vanilla. When thickened, remove lemon peel.

3. In a flat baking dish, arrange alternate layers of this mixture with spongecake fingers and peaches. End with a cream layer on top.

4. Whip cream; add brandy, confectioners' sugar, and nutmeg. Spread on top of cake layer. Chill 4 to 8 hours.

"Prayer, fasting and all other Christian undertakings are good in themselves; however, the performing of these things is not the end of our life because they are only the means. The true goal of the Christian life is to acquire the Holy Spirit."

—Saint Seraphim of Sarov

Whitsun Cake

Ingredients

2/3 cup milk
1 cup sugar
1¹/3 cups flour, sifted
3 teaspoons baking powder
2 egg whites
¹/4 teaspoon cream of tartar

¹/4 teaspoon salt
1 teaspoon vanilla
15 large strawberries
1¹/2 cups confectioners' sugar
2 tablespoons butter or margarine

1. Preheat oven to 350°.

2. Scald milk and allow it to cool. Sift sugar, flour, and baking powder together 3 times. Add cooled milk gradually, beating constantly.

3. Beat egg whites with cream of tartar, salt, and vanilla 1¹/2 to 2 minutes, or until the egg whites refuse to slip when the bowl is tipped. Fold into flour mixture.

4. Bake in an ungreased 7-inch tube pan for 45 minutes, or until the cake is golden brown and firm to the touch. Invert the cake on a rack until cool.

5. Hull and clean the strawberries. Crush 8 berries with a fork, and sweeten to taste. Cream the butter or margarine and confectioners' sugar in a bowl, then add enough crushed berries and juice to make a mixture of spreading consistency. Frost the cake and top with 7 whole strawberries as a reminder of the gifts of the Holy Spirit.

"Why did Christ refer to the grace of the Spirit under the name of water? Because through water all vegetables and animals live. Because the water of rain comes down from heaven, and though rain comes down in one form, its effects take many forms. Yea, one spring watered all of paradise, and the same rain falls on the whole world, yet it becomes white in the lily, red in the rose, purple in the violet."

—Saint Cyril of Jerusalem

Summer

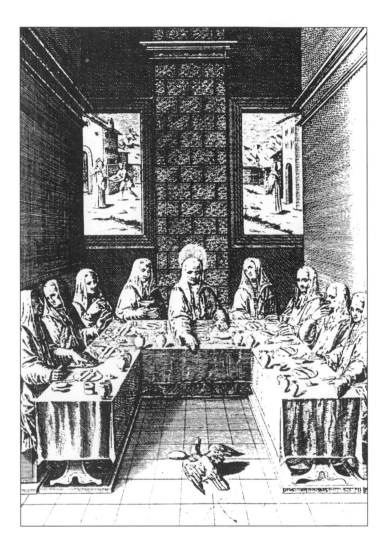

"To love Christ above all else"

—Rule of Saint Benedict, Chapter 4

Parsley Soup

(Potage au persil)

Ingredients   *4 servings*

3 medium tomatoes

4 tablespoons olive oil

1 leek, finely chopped

1 onion, chopped and minced

4 1/2 cups water

3 garlic cloves, minced

1 cup dry white wine

1 big bunch parsley, finely chopped

salt and pepper to taste

1. Boil the tomatoes for 5 minutes, cool them in cold water, and then peel. Slice lengthwise and discard the pulp and seeds.

2. Pour the olive oil into a soup pot, then add the leek and the onion; sauté until they begin to brown. Add the tomatoes, garlic, wine, water, salt, and pepper. Boil over low to medium heat for 20 minutes. Add the parsley and continue cooking the soup for another 10 minutes.

3. Process soup in a blender. Serve hot or refrigerate for a few hours and serve cold.

They said of Abba Macarius the Great that he became, as it is written, a god upon earth because just as God protects the world, so Abba Macarius would cover the faults that he saw as though he did not see them, and those which he heard as though he did not hear them.

—from *Sayings of the Desert Fathers*

Quick Vichyssoise

Ingredients   *4–6 servings*

4 tablespoons butter or margarine

4 leeks, finely sliced

4 potatoes, diced

3 bouillon cubes (or use vegetable stock in place of water)

1 bouquet garni (1 bay leaf, 1 thyme sprig, and 1 parsley sprig tied together)

2 cups milk

2 cups water

1 cup heavy cream

salt and fresh pepper to taste

fresh parsley or mint leaves for optional garnish

1. Melt the butter or margarine in a large soup pot. Add the leeks and cook over low heat for 5 to 6 minutes, or until tender. Add the potatoes, bouillon, bouquet garni, milk, salt, pepper, and water (you may add more water if desired).

2. Raise the heat to medium and allow the soup to cook slowly for 25 to 30 minutes. Turn down the heat and simmer the soup for an additional 10 minutes. Remove the bouquet garni and process the soup in a blender until smooth.

3. Chill the soup for a few hours, and just before serving, add the heavy cream and stir thoroughly. Garnish the soup with finely chopped parsley or mint leaves if you wish.

"All guests who arrive to the monastery should be welcomed as Christ, because he will say, 'I was a stranger and you took me in.' Show them every courtesy, especially to servants of God and pilgrims."

—from the Holy Rule of Saint Benedict

Saint Macarius Cucumbers

(Concombres Saint-Macaire)

Ingredients   *2 servings*

2 cucumbers   chervil and coriander, finely chopped
6 tablespoons low-fat yogurt   salt
1 lemon

1. Peel the cucumbers and cut in thin slices, letting them soak in cold salted water for 3 hours. Rinse the cucumbers in cold water and drain thoroughly.

2. Combine the yogurt, lemon juice, chervil, and coriander. Mix well. Pour over the cucumbers and toss gently. Serve cold.

Saint Macarius the Elder was a desert monk who lived in Egypt from the years A.D. 300 to 390. Following the example of Saint Antony the Great, he withdrew into the wilderness when he was thirty years old and stayed there another six decades. He was renowned for his silent and austere life and for his wisdom. Because he was one of the first monks to retire to the desert, he is rightly considered to be one of the fathers of early monasticism.

Bread Pissaladière

1 cup olive oil
1 onion, sliced
15 ounces pitted black olives
4 tablespoons herbs provençales
   (basil, thyme, rosemary)

4 ripe tomatoes, sliced
1 loaf French bread, sliced
garlic cloves and anchovies (optional)
grated cheese (optional)

1. Preheat oven to 400°.

2. Pour the olive oil into a blender; add the onion, black olives, and herbs (garlic and anchovies, if desired), and blend thoroughly until smooth.

3. Cover the slices of bread with the spread (about 4 slices per person), and place on a greased or oiled baking sheet.

4. Arrange the tomatoes on top. If you wish, sprinkle some herbs or grated cheese on the tomatoes. Bake for 15 minutes, or under the broiler for a few minutes, until the tomatoes are cooked. Serve as appetizers or canapés before dinner. This is especially good in midsummer when tomatoes are in season.

"We are going to establish a school for God's service. In founding it we hope to introduce nothing harsh or burdensome. For preserving charity or correcting faults, it may be necessary at times, by reason of justice, to be slightly more severe. Do not fear this and retreat, for the path to salvation is long and the entrance is narrow."

—from the Holy Rule of Saint Benedict

Tuna Mousse

Ingredients   *4 servings*

1 envelope unflavored gelatin
2 tablespoons lemon juice
1/2 cup boiling chicken broth
   or an all-vegetable broth
1/2 cup mayonnaise
1/4 cup milk
2 tablespoons parsley, chopped

1 teaspoon dried dill (fresh
   dill is even better)
1 teaspoon Dijon mustard
1/4 teaspoon white pepper
7 ounces tuna, drained and flaked
1 cup cucumber, shredded

1. In a deep mixing bowl, soften the gelatin in the lemon juice. Add the boiling broth and stir to dissolve the gelatin.

2. Add the remaining ingredients, except the tuna and the cucumber, and mix everything well. Chill for about 30 minutes, until slightly thickened. Fold in the tuna and cucumber and beat until mixture turns frothy.

3. Pour the mixture into a serving bowl or mold and chill until firm. Serve cold.

A brother asked Abba Poemen, "Is it better to speak or be silent?" The old man said to him, "One who speaks for God's sake does well; but one who is silent for God's sake also does well."

—from *Sayings of the Desert Fathers*

Cauliflower Santa Lucia

Ingredients

1 head cauliflower
3 tablespoons butter
2 carrots, diced
1 onion, finely chopped

1 cup white vermouth or white wine
salt and pepper to taste
dash dried mustard
finely grated cheese of your choice

1. Preheat oven to 350°.

2. Separate the cauliflower florets. Slice the stems in 1-inch pieces. Melt the butter into a large skillet; add the cauliflower, carrots, and onion. Sauté the vegetables for about 3 minutes. Add the vermouth or wine, salt and pepper, mustard, and continue cooking over medium heat for another 3 minutes.

3. Butter a baking dish that has a lid. Place the vegetable mixture in it. Cover the dish and bake for 20 minutes.

4. Sprinkle on the finely grated cheese and continue baking for another 10 minutes. Serve hot.

"They cannot be deemed worthy of the kingdom of heaven who do not imitate in their relations with one another the equality which is observed by children among themselves."

—from the Short Rules of Saint Basil

Potato and Carrot Puff

Ingredients   *6 servings*

8 large potatoes
6 large carrots
6 tablespoons butter
4 egg yolks

1 cup milk
salt and pepper to taste
4 egg whites

1. Preheat oven to 350°.

2. Wash and peel the potatoes and carrots. Boil until done, then drain; add the butter and mash together thoroughly.

3. Beat the egg yolks and milk in a deep bowl. Add the mashed potatoes, carrots, salt, and pepper and mix well.

4. Beat the egg whites until stiff. Fold the beaten whites into the potato-carrot mixture. Grease a baking dish well and pour the mixture into it. Bake for 20 to 25 minutes, until the top turns golden brown. Serve hot.

"O light that never fades, as the light of day now streams through these windows and floods this room, so let me open to You the windows of my heart, that all my life may be filled by the radiance of Your presence....Let there be nothing within me to darken the brightness of the day."

—John Baillie

Avocado Omelette

(Omelette à l'avocat)

Ingredients　　　　　　　　　　　　　　　　　　　　　　　　　　*2 servings*

5 eggs　　　　　　　　　　　　　　1 firm avocado
salt and pepper to taste　　　　　　olive oil
pinch of chervil, finely chopped

1. Break the eggs into a bowl and beat vigorously. Add salt and pepper and chervil, and beat some more.

2. Peel the avocado and dice in cubes. Pour sufficient oil into an omelette pan and heat. When the oil is hot, place the avocado in the pan, stir, and cook for a few seconds. Pour the egg mixture on top and cook, lifting the edges with a spatula to permit the uncooked egg to run under.

3. When one side of the omelette is done, carefully fold in half. (Do not overcook, since the omelette should remain moist inside.) Slide the omelette onto a previously warmed plate and serve immediately.

"He prayeth best who loveth best
All things both great and small;
For the dear God who loveth us,
He made and loveth all."

—Samuel Taylor Coleridge in
"The Rime of the Ancient Mariner"

Egg Noodles with Basil and Cheese

Ingredients

6 servings

1 pound egg noodles
4 tablespoons butter
4 tablespoons olive oil
1 cup fresh basil, thinly chopped

4 garlic cloves, finely chopped
3/4 cup grated Romano
  or Parmesan cheese
salt and fresh pepper to taste

1. In a large pot, bring 4 quarts of salted water to a boil. Add the noodles. Cook for about 10 minutes, stirring from time to time, then drain.

2. Sauté the basil and garlic in the butter and olive oil for a minute or two.

3. Combine all the ingredients in a casserole dish and serve hot, with additional cheese on the side for those who wish to add more.

NOTE: This simple and appetizing recipe can be adapted to any kind of pasta or noodles.

"In the deserts of the heart
Let the healing fountain start;
In the prison of his days
Teach the free man how to praise."

—W. H. Auden

Vegetable-Cheese Casserole

Ingredients   *8 servings*

2 medium eggplants (or 1 large)
3 cups milk
6 eggs, well beaten
2 teaspoons cornstarch
1 small onion, chopped

8 ounces frozen spinach,
   thawed, drained, and chopped
salt, pepper, dash of nutmeg
bread slices seasoned with garlic
Cheddar cheese, coarsely grated

1. Preheat oven to 350°.

2. Slice and parboil eggplants. Combine all other ingredients except bread and cheese.

3. Butter a large casserole dish. Fill with alternating layers: milk mixture (on bottom), bread slices, milk mixture, cheese, eggplant slices. Repeat layers ending with milk mixture and cheese on top. Bake until heated through, about 1 hour.

"Pride is to stick to one's own judgment, without taking into account God's transforming creative love."

—Mother Maria

Spinach Casserole with Tomato Topping

Ingredients

6 servings

White Sauce

6 tablespoons butter

6 tablespoons flour

3 cups milk

$1\frac{1}{2}$ teaspoons salt

$\frac{1}{8}$ teaspoon pepper

dash nutmeg

4 eggs, beaten

$1\frac{1}{2}$ to 2 cups stale whole wheat bread, cubed

16 ounces frozen spinach, thawed, drained, and chopped (or equivalent fresh spinach)

sliced Cheddar cheese

Topping

2 to 3 fresh tomatoes

1 large onion, chopped

oregano and parsley

salt and pepper

1. Make white sauce according to directions on page 146. Season with nutmeg. Add eggs, bread, and spinach, and mix thoroughly.

2. Place the mixture in a buttered casserole dish. Cover with sliced cheese.

3. Preheat oven to 350°.

4. Cut tomatoes into thick slices and fry briefly with chopped onion, oregano, parsley, salt, and pepper. Place tomato slices and seasonings on top of casserole. Bake until bubbly and browned, about 1 hour.

"Be merry, really merry. The life of the true Christian should be perpetual jubilee—a prelude to the festivals of eternity."

—Saint Theophane Vernard

Creamed Mushrooms on Toast

(Farce aux champignons)

Ingredients 6 servings

1/2 pound mushrooms, washed and sliced

2 tablespoons butter

1 tablespoon olive oil

1/4 cup onion or shallot, diced

salt and pepper

garlic powder (optional)

6 slices toast

White Sauce

4 tablespoons butter

4 tablespoons flour

2 cups milk

salt and pepper to taste

1. Sauté mushrooms with the butter and olive oil until they begin to brown; add onion, salt, pepper, and optional garlic powder, and continue sautéing gently until onion is transparent.

2. Make a white sauce according to directions on page 146. Season to taste. Stir mushrooms and onions into sauce.

3. Serve sauce over slices of toast. You may wish to place sauce-covered toast under a broiler for a few minutes, until sauce is bubbly and slightly brown on top.

"The flow of prayer is like the Gulf Stream, imparting warmth to all that is cold, melting all that is hard to life."

—Abraham Joshua Heschel

Tivoli Corn Scallop

Ingredients   *6–8 servings*

2 eggs
17 ounces cream-style corn
1/2 cup soda crackers, crushed
1/4 cup undiluted evaporated milk
1/4 cup green pepper, chopped
1 teaspoon onion, chopped
1/2 teaspoon sugar
1/4 cup butter or margarine, melted

1/4 cup carrot, finely shredded
1 tablespoon celery, chopped
6 drops Tabasco sauce
1/2 teaspoon salt
1/2 cup shredded Cheddar cheese
paprika
1/4 cup sesame seeds (optional)

1. Preheat oven to 350°.

2. In large bowl, beat eggs with fork. Add the remaining ingredients, except cheese, paprika, and sesame seeds, and mix thoroughly. Put in a greased 8-inch square baking dish. Sprinkle with cheese and paprika. Bake for 30 minutes, or until mixture is set and top is golden brown. (A sprinkling of sesame seeds gives a nice crunch.)

"The past must be abandoned to God's mercy, the present to our fidelity, and the future to divine providence."

—Saint Francis de Sales

Cloister Carrots

Ingredients   *6–8 servings*

10 large carrots   ¹/₂ cup blanched, slivered almonds
2 tablespoons brown sugar   1 quart milk
1 cup raisins

1. Wash and peel the carrots; cut in very thin slices.

2. In a pot, combine the carrots, brown sugar, raisins, and almonds with the milk.

3. Bring to a boil and then simmer for 1 hour, stirring occasionally. Serve hot in the winter or chill and serve cold in the summer.

"It may be objected that the monastic movement attempted to cure economic evils by running away from them, and that the monk's cell provided a last refuge for those who 'had despaired of the state.' This is very far from the case. The monastic movement …made an honest endeavor to correct in the world at large the results of an economic system which it could not alter."

—E. F. Morison, Oxford

Sautéed Zucchini

Ingredients   *4–6 servings*

4 medium-size zucchinis
1/2 cup oil or butter
2 tablespoons scallions
   or shallots, chopped

2 tablespoons parsley, chopped
salt and fresh pepper to taste

1. Wash zucchinis and cut into sticks without peeling or removing the seeds. Boil in salted water for 2 minutes. Drain.

2. Just before serving, pour the oil (olive oil is best) or melt the butter in a pan and add the zucchini immediately. Add chopped scallions, parsley, salt, and pepper. Sauté 5 minutes and serve when warm and tender.

"Do not in spirit become discontented, for discontent lodges in the bosom of a fool. Do not say: How is it that former times were better than these? For it is not in wisdom that you ask this….On a good day enjoy the good things, and on an evil day consider: both the one and the other God has made."

—Ecclesiastes 7:9–10,14

Toledo Spanish Tuna

Ingredients   *4 servings*

1/4 cup oil of choice
1 cup rice
1 medium onion, thinly sliced
1/3 cup green pepper, chopped
1 garlic clove, minced
20 ounces canned tomatoes
1/2 cup tomato juice

1 1/2 cups water
8 ounces sliced or canned mushrooms
1 teaspoon salt
dash of cayenne
7 ounces chunk-style tuna,
    drained and flaked

1. Heat oil in a saucepan or large skillet. Add rice. Sauté until golden. Add onions, green pepper, garlic clove, tomatoes, tomato juice, water, mushrooms, salt, and cayenne.

2. Cook, covered, over low heat for 35 to 40 minutes, or until rice is done, stirring occasionally. Add tuna. Cover and heat thoroughly. Serve hot.

"Meditation with great mental industry plods along the steep and laborious road, keeping the end in view. Contemplation on a free wing circles around with great nimbleness wherever the impulse takes it. Meditation investigates; contemplation wonders."

—Richard of Saint Victor

Scalloped Fish Sainte-Mélanie

Ingredients   *4 servings*

1½ pounds fish fillets
10 ¾ ounces condensed
  mushroom soup
2 tablespoons green pepper, diced
1 can green peas, drained
¼ cup lemon juice

salt and pepper to taste
dash of Worcestershire sauce
4 slices bread, lightly toasted and cubed
¼ cup butter, melted
grated cheese of your choice (optional
  substitute for buttered bread cubes)

1. Preheat oven to 350°.

2. Cut fish fillets into ½-inch cubes. Combine with all other ingredients, except bread cubes, butter, and cheese, and place in well-greased baking dish.

3. Cover with bread cubes that have been mixed with melted butter, or sprinkle with grated cheese. Bake until heated through and brown on top, about 1 hour.

"Don't think of God as a very stern judge and punisher. He is very merciful….We must not despair, for there is no sin that exceeds God's compassion. It is always the devil that brings despair; one must not listen to him."

—letter from a Russian monk

Spinach Crêpes

Crêpes
2 eggs
1 cup flour

1 cup milk

Filling
3 tablespoons butter
1 onion, chopped
2 garlic cloves, minced

1 bunch fresh spinach, washed, dried,
    and chopped (or 8 ounces frozen
    spinach, thawed, drained, and chopped)
4 eggs, hard-boiled and chopped
1 cup Cheddar cheese, coarsely grated

Cream Sauce
3 tablespoons butter
3 tablespoons flour
1 1/2 cups milk

dash nutmeg
salt and pepper

1. Make crêpe batter by beating the 2 eggs thoroughly. Then beat in the flour. Stir in 1 cup milk. Put the batter in the refrigerator to rest while you prepare the filling.

2. In a nonaluminum pan (aluminum tends to blacken spinach and/or make it taste bitter and acidic), melt butter. Gently sauté (*don't brown*) the onion, then add garlic and chopped spinach. If fresh spinach is used, cover for about 2 minutes to wilt it down. Turn off heat. Add chopped eggs and cheese.

3. Preheat oven to 300°. Make thin crêpes, according to directions on page 50. Make a white sauce following method on page 146. Place a spoonful of the filling on each crêpe, roll up, and arrange in baking dish. Cover with sauce. Bake for 15 minutes.

"A good name is better than ointment, and the day of death than the day of birth….Better is the end of speech than its beginning; better is the patient spirit than the lofty spirit."

—Ecclesiastes 7:1,8

Green and Beet Salad

Ingredients

1¹/₂ pounds medium-size beets
1 head romaine lettuce
¹/₃ cup olive oil
2 tablespoons apple cider vinegar

¹/₂ teaspoon salt
¹/₂ teaspoon freshly ground pepper
2 tablespoons scallions, chopped
1 tablespoon Dijon mustard

1. Cut the tops off the beets and put the beets in a pan with boiling water. Cook for 30 minutes, or until tender. Drain and cool, then peel and cut into thin slices.

2. Tear the romaine into bite-size pieces and mix with the beet slices. Combine the oil, vinegar, salt, pepper, scallions, and mustard. Mix well and pour over the beets and lettuce. Serve.

"I God am in your midst.
Whoever knows me can never fall.
Not in the height, nor in the depth, nor in the breadth.
For I am love, that the vast expanses of evil can never still."

—Saint Hildegard of Bingen

Italian Corn Salad

(Salade de maïs Italienne)

Ingredients   *4 servings*

1 green pepper, thinly sliced   12 ounces canned corn
1 red pepper, thinly sliced   3 tablespoons parsley, minced
2 red onions, thinly sliced

Vinaigrette
6 tablespoons olive oil   salt and pepper to taste
3 tablespoons wine vinegar

1. Wash and slice the peppers and onions. Place them in a large salad bowl. Drain the corn thoroughly and mix with the onions and peppers.

2. Prepare a simple vinaigrette by mixing the olive oil, vinegar, salt, and pepper. Pour the vinaigrette over the salad and mix well.

3. Refrigerate for 30 minutes. Sprinkle the parsley on top of the salad before serving.

"Oh how an ignorant and simple soul, who knows only how to love God without loving self, surpasses all the learned! The Spirit intimates all truth to it without detailed study; for by an intimate, profound enlightenment, an enlightenment of truth, experience, and feeling, it makes it realize that it itself is nothing and that God is everything."

—J. B. Bossuet

Fennel Salad

(Fenouil en salade)

Ingredients

4 servings

4 fresh fennel bulbs

1 red onion, thinly sliced

4 ripe medium tomatoes, quartered

hard-boiled eggs as garnish (optional)

Dressing

$1/2$ cup olive oil

juice of one lemon

6 tablespoons tarragon vinegar

3 tablespoons fresh coriander,

finely chopped (or parsley)

salt and fresh pepper to taste

1. Trim off and discard the stems and outer skin of fennel bulbs. Cook them in boiling water for exactly 30 minutes. Rinse fennel in cold water and allow it to cool, then cut into quarters.

2. Place the quartered fennel into a salad bowl. Add the onion and the tomatoes.

3. Combine the dressing ingredients according to directions on page 151. Pour over the salad and toss before serving.

NOTE: Crumbled hard-boiled eggs are an attractive garnish for this salad.

"Better is a dish of herbs where love is than a fattened ox and hatred with it."

—Proverbs 15:17

Fresh Mushroom and Watercress Salad

1 tablespoon Dijon mustard
  (French, preferably)
1/4 cup olive oil
2 tablespoons apple cider vinegar
3 tablespoons scallions, chopped

salt and pepper to taste
1/2 pound fresh mushrooms
1 bunch watercress
1 head romaine lettuce

1. Place mustard and olive oil in a bowl and mix thoroughly with a wire whisk. Add the vinegar, scallions, salt, and pepper, and whisk again. Clean the mushrooms, slice thinly, and mix with the dressing. Chill until ready to use.

2. Wash and drain well both the watercress and romaine lettuce. Break into bite-size pieces. When ready to serve the salad, pour the dressing over it and mix well.

"It is written: 'An altar of earth thou shalt make unto Me…and if thou make Me an altar of stone, thou shalt not build it of hewn stones, for if thou lift up thy tool upon it, thou hast profaned it.' The altar of earth is the altar of silence, which pleases God beyond all else. But if you make an altar of words, do not hew and chisel them, for such artifice would profane it."

—Hasidic saying

Tutti-Frutti Salad

Ingredients   *8 servings*

1 ripe melon (any kind), diced
2 pears, sliced
2 apples, sliced
1 orange, diced
1 banana, sliced (optional)

1/2 cup seedless raisins
1/3 cup brown sugar
4 teaspoons lemon juice
1/2 cup Porto wine or another sweet wine

1. Mix all of the fruits in a large salad bowl with the sugar and lemon juice. Refrigerate for at least 1 hour.

2. Just before serving, pour the Porto wine over the fruit and mix thoroughly. Serve cold.

"We should not be eager to have the necessities of life in abundance, nor seek after luxury or satiety; but we should be free from every form of avarice and ostentation."

—from the Short Rules of Saint Basil

DESSERTS

Millbrook Prune Pudding

Ingredients

1/2 pound prunes
13/4 cups stale bread crumbs
1/3 cup brown sugar
4 tablespoons butter

1/4 cup cognac
2 tablespoons lemon juice
1/2 cup prune juice

1. Cook the prunes until they are tender. Cool, pit, and slice them in halves.

2. Grease a 9-inch square baking dish well and carefully arrange layers of stale bread crumbs (use 3/4 cup per layer), sliced prunes, sugar, and small dots of butter. Repeat. Cover the top with remaining 1/4 cup dried crumbs and what is left of the butter.

3. Preheat oven to 375°. Pour cognac, lemon juice, and prune juice into a container. Shake and mix thoroughly. Pour this liquid over the pudding mixture. Bake for 35 to 40 minutes. Allow to cool before serving.

"We should not be vacillating but steadfast in the faith and staunch in cleaving to the good things which are in the Lord."

—from the Short Rules of Saint Basil

Melon with Strawberries and Anisette

(Melon à l'anisette et aux fraises)

Ingredients   *4 servings*

2 cantaloupe melons   4 tablespoons anisette
1/2 cup sugar   32 fresh strawberries

1. Peel the melons and remove the seeds. Cut in small slices and mash into a purée. Add the sugar and the anisette and mix everything thoroughly. Refrigerate for at least 2 hours.

2. Spoon the purée into chilled glass dishes and arrange whole strawberries on the top.

NOTE: This is a quick and easy dessert to prepare on a hot summer day.

"If there is righteousness in the heart, there will be beauty in the character. If there is beauty in the character, there will be harmony in the home. If there is harmony in the home, there will be order in the nation. When there is order in the nation, there will be peace on earth."

—Sathya Sai Baba

Peach and Banana Sorbet

Ingredients *6–8 servings*

4 cups sugar
4 cups water
2 teaspoons vanilla
4 cups peaches, sliced

2 ripe bananas
juice of 4 lemons
juice of 4 oranges
2 tablespoons peach liqueur

1. Stir and dissolve the sugar in the water over low to medium heat. Stir in the vanilla; remove from heat and cool completely.

2. Purée the peaches and bananas in a blender or food processor. Add the lemon and orange juices and liqueur to the cooled syrup and combine with the fruit purée in the blender. Process only to mix well. (Work in two batches if necessary.)

3. Divide the sorbet into 6 or 8 individual molds or serving dishes and freeze until ready to be served.

NOTE: This dessert is easy to prepare and especially pleasant during the hot summer months.

"There is but one point in the universe where God communicates with us, and that is the center of our own soul."

—Archbishop Ullathorne

Peach or Pear Compote

Ingredients   *6 servings*

2 pounds peaches   1 tablespoon white wine or
3/4 cup water   any liqueur (optional)
1 1/4 cups sugar

1. Peel peaches, remove pits, and cut in half.

2. Heat water and sugar together. When sugar is completely dissolved, add peaches. Simmer over low heat for about 15 minutes.

3. To enhance taste, add 1 tablespoon white wine or your favorite liqueur.

Ingredients   *6 servings*

2 pounds pears   1 1/4 cups wine (white, preferably)
1 cup sugar (or more)   1 tablespoon rum
3/4 cup water

1. If the pears are small, peel and leave whole. If they are larger, peel and cut in halves or quarters and remove seeds.

2. Bring the sugar, wine, and water to a boil, stirring constantly. Remove from the heat as soon as it begins to boil. Add the pears. Cook gently for about 20 minutes.

3. Refrigerate for at least 1 hour. Just before serving, add 1 tablespoon rum to the compote.

"Oh, how happy are the alleluias of heaven! Here below we sing it in anxiety and pain; up there we will sing it in peace!"

—Saint Augustine

Barrytown Apple Crumble

Ingredients

6 servings

4 to 6 apples, sliced
1 cup flour
1/2 cup sugar
1 teaspoon baking powder

1/4 teaspoon salt
2 eggs
3 tablespoons butter or margarine

1. Preheat oven to 375°.

2. Arrange apple slices in a 9-inch round cake pan. Mix all other ingredients, except butter or margarine, until crumbly, and sprinkle over the top.

3. Drizzle with melted butter. Bake for 30 minutes or until apples are done.

"For we shall see verily in heaven, without end, that we have grievously sinned in this life, and notwithstanding this, we shall see that we were never hurt in God's love, nor were of less price in God's sight. For hard and marvelous is that love which may not, nor will not, be broken for trespass."

—Julian of Norwich

Yogurt Cake Saint-Elie

Ingredients

3 cups flour, sifted
2 cups sugar
1 teaspoon baking powder
   (double if whole wheat flour is used)

3 eggs
1 cup natural yogurt*
1 teaspoon vanilla
³/₄ cup oil

1. Preheat oven to 350°.

2. Butter and flour an 8-inch square cake pan. Combine dry ingredients.

3. Beat eggs thoroughly. Beat in yogurt, vanilla, and oil; add dry ingredients.

4. Pour batter into baking pan. Bake about 50 minutes.

*Avoid yogurts containing stabilizers. If you can get natural yogurt with fruits, etc., they will work; decrease sugar if yogurt is sweetened.

"Readings, vigils and prayer—these are the things that lend stability to the wandering mind."

—Evagrius Ponticus

Autumn

"As our lives and faith progress, the heart expands and with the sweetness of love we move down the paths of God's commandments. Never departing from His guidance, remaining in the monastery until death, we patiently share in Christ's passion, so we may eventually enter the Kingdom of God."

—Conclusion of the Prologue to the Rule of Saint Benedict

Soup Julienne

(Potage Julienne au bouillon)

Ingredients   *6 servings*

3 leeks (white part only)   3 quarts water
4 carrots   3 bouillon cubes
2 medium turnips   salt and pepper to taste
1/2 medium head green cabbage   1/3 cup fresh parsley, minced
1 onion

1. Shred the cabbage and cut the vegetables in thin strips, 11/2 inches long, and place them in a large soup pot with the water. Add the bouillon cubes and bring the water to boil. Reduce the heat to medium, cover, and cook the soup slowly for about 45 minutes, stirring from time to time.

2. When the vegetables are done, add the salt, pepper, and parsley; stir a few times, cover, and simmer for 15 additional minutes. Serve hot.

"A person can show his religion as much in measuring onions as he can in singing 'Glory hallelujah!'"

—Shaker brother

Escarole Soup

Ingredients   *6 servings*

1½ pounds escarole,   3 bouillon cubes
   coarsely chopped   ½ cup vermicelli noodles or
1 onion, finely chopped   any other small pasta
3 garlic cloves, minced   salt and pepper to taste
6 tablespoons olive oil   grated cheese of your choice (optional)
2 quarts water

1. Sauté the garlic and onion in the oil in a large kettle for 3 to 4 minutes. Add the escarole and stir so that the oil is evenly distributed.

2. Add the water and the bouillon and cook over medium heat, covered, for 15 minutes. Then add the vermicelli noodles, salt, and pepper, and continue cooking for another 10 minutes, stirring occasionally.

3. Turn off the heat, and with the lid in place, allow the soup to rest for an additional 10 minutes before serving. Sprinkle grated cheese on top of each serving if you wish.

"No spiritual exercise can be compared to that of silence for those who wish to acquire inner peace."

—Saint Seraphim of Sarov

Basic Monastic Garlic Soup

Ingredients   *6 servings*

16 large garlic cloves, minced
4 tablespoons olive oil (or more)
1 cup dry white wine
6 cups bouillon
salt to taste

1/4 teaspoon nutmeg
6 slices whole wheat bread
3 egg yolks, beaten
3 egg whites, stiffly beaten

1. Sauté the garlic in olive oil in a soup pot for a few minutes. Add the wine, bouillon, salt, and nutmeg, and bring to boil.

2. Reduce the heat to low to medium, add the egg yolks, and cook for 15 minutes. Simmer for another 15 minutes, covered.

3. Place one slice of bread in each of six soup plates. Scatter the stiff egg whites over the bread. Ladle the hot soup over the bread and serve immediately.

"Sing as travelers sing: sing and walk! Not to pamper laziness but to maintain strength. Sing and walk! As you walk, advance in good works, advance in upright faith, advance in a pure life without going astray, without backsliding, without stopping. Sing and walk!"

—Saint Augustine

Lentil and Lemon Peel Soup

Ingredients   *4–6 servings*

1 cup lentils   2 bouillon cubes
6 cups water   4 tablespoons olive oil
1 onion, finely chopped   salt and pepper
4 garlic cloves, minced   peel of 1/2 lemon, grated

1. Combine all ingredients in a large pot and simmer until lentils are tender, about 1 1/2 hours.

2. Stir occasionally and check to see that there is enough liquid to prevent burning. Serve hot.

"One must never forget that on the human side a monastic life is the desert; on the spiritual side, the communion of saints in heaven."

—Mother Maria

Zucchini Stuffed Tomatoes

Ingredients   *8 servings*

8 medium tomatoes, halved
1 medium zucchini, grated
1 small onion, chopped
3 garlic cloves, minced
6 basil leaves, chopped
2 parsley sprigs, chopped

1/4 teaspoon thyme
4 teaspoons olive oil
2 teaspoons grated cheese
   (Parmesan or other)
salt and pepper to taste

1. Preheat oven to 300°. Cut a hole on the top of each tomato. Carefully scoop out the pulp and lace it with a fork in a deep bowl.

2. Place the zucchini, onion, garlic, basil, parsley, and tomato pulp in a food processor and mix. Return the vegetable mixture to the deep bowl. Add the thyme, olive oil, grated cheese, salt, and pepper, and mix all the ingredients thoroughly.

3. Fill and stuff the tomatoes with the mixture. Butter or grease well a flat ovenproof dish and carefully place the tomatoes in it. Bake for 30 minutes. Serve the tomatoes hot.

"Union with God can never be anything but the accord of two distinct wills, and therefore, this union with God can be effected in no other way than through love."

—Bernard of Clairvaux

Vegetable Fritters

Ingredients   *6 servings*

1 long and rather thin eggplant, sliced   pancake mix
1 long zucchini, sliced   olive oil or oil of choice
1 long yellow squash, sliced   salt to taste
2 fennel bulbs, sliced

1. Wash and thoroughly clean the vegetables. Slice them evenly, not too thick.

2. Prepare the pancake batter, following the instructions on the package. Coat the sliced vegetables with the batter and fry them in hot oil, a few at a time (both sides), until they become dry and crisp. Place them on a paper towel to drain. Serve hot.

"Sympathy with those who have fallen is the best way of not falling oneself."

—Saint Philip Neri

Eggs Cocotte

(Oeufs cocotte)

Ingredients   *6 servings*

    1¹/₂ cups heavy cream   salt and pepper to taste
    6 eggs

1. Preheat oven to 350°.

2. Put 2 tablespoons heavy cream in each of six ramekins and place in ovenproof saucepan or skillet. Add water to come halfway up the side of the bowls, but do not let the water get inside the bowls.

3. Boil the water for exactly 2 minutes, and then break an egg into each of the bowls and cover the top with 2 more tablespoons of heavy cream. Sprinkle salt and pepper on each egg and place the entire saucepan, with ramekins in it, in oven for about 6 minutes. Serve immediately.

NOTE: This simple dish may be used as an introduction to a good meal, or it is a nutritious lunch or light supper by itself.

"In the midst of our work we can fulfill the duty of prayer, giving thanks to him who has granted strength to our hands for performing our tasks and cleverness to our minds for acquiring knowledge, and for providing the materials."

—from the Long Rules of Saint Basil

Cauliflower Fritters

Ingredients

4 servings

1 head cauliflower
1 egg, beaten lightly
1/2 cup milk
3/4 cup flour

3/4 cup grated cheese of your choice
pinch of salt
oil of choice for deep frying

1. Cook the whole cauliflower in lightly salted water in a deep saucepan for 5 to 6 minutes. It should remain firm. Separate the cauliflower into florets and put in colander to ensure that excess water drains off.

2. Combine beaten egg, milk, flour, cheese, and salt, and beat until creamy and smooth. Let the batter rest for at least an hour before using it.

3. Dip each floret into the batter and fry in hot, deep oil. Serve hot.

"The human heart lies open to God alone, for it is a fathomless depth."

—Saint Seraphim of Sarov

Butternut Squash with Garlic

Ingredients   *4–6 servings*

5 butternut squashes
4 ounces butter or 1/2 cup oil of choice
6 large garlic cloves, finely minced

salt and freshly ground pepper to taste
parsley, finely chopped (optional)

1. Wash and peel the squash; remove the seeds; cut into 2-inch cubes. Cover with water and boil 5 to 7 minutes, being careful not to overcook. Cubes should remain firm. Drain.

2. In a large skillet, melt the butter or heat oil, add the garlic cloves, and sauté for 1 minute. Do not allow the garlic to brown or burn.

3. Place the squash cubes in a serving bowl and pour the melted butter or oil and garlic over them. Sprinkle with salt and pepper, and gently toss the vegetables. Finely chopped parsley makes an attractive garnish. Serve immediately.

"Work is to be undertaken, not merely for the sake of keeping the body under subjection, but also for showing love to our neighbor, in order that through us God may provide a sufficiency for those brethren who are in want."

—from the Long Rules of Saint Basil

Broccoli with Hollandaise Sauce

Ingredients

4 servings

4 large broccoli stems

Hollandaise Sauce

1/2 cup melted butter
3 egg yolks
1 tablespoon lemon juice
1/2 teaspoon salt

1/4 teaspoon white pepper
dash of nutmeg
1/3 cup boiling water

1. Wash the broccoli stems and cut in four pieces lengthwise. Trim the ends. Cook until the stalks are tender.

2. Meanwhile, prepare a hollandaise sauce in the top of a double boiler by whisking the melted butter and adding one egg yolk at a time. Add lemon juice, salt, pepper, and nutmeg while continuing to whisk.

3. Just before serving, place over boiling water and add, little by little, 1/3 cup of boiling water to the sauce, constantly stirring, until the sauce thickens. To prevent further cooking, separate pan with sauce from lower part of double boiler.

4. Drain the broccoli, salt to taste, and serve with hollandaise sauce.

"Nothing should alienate us from one another, but that which alienates us from God."

—Benjamin Whichcote

Saint Hubert Fish Stew

Ingredients   *6 servings*

2 onions, chopped
4 garlic cloves, minced
6 tablespoons oil of choice
1 pound cod or similar fish
4 carrots, sliced
2 parsnips, sliced

3 potatoes, diced
4 tablespoons parsley, chopped
1 bay leaf
2 bottles beer
4 cups water
salt and white pepper to taste

1. Sauté the onion and garlic in the oil in a stew pot for a few minutes.

2. Add the remaining ingredients, stir well, cover, and cook slowly over low to medium heat for 35 to 40 minutes. Stir from time to time so that the stew does not burn at the bottom. Serve hot.

"Then only is our life a whole, when work and contemplation dwell in us side by side, and we are perfectly in both of them at once."

—Ruysbroeck

Lentils and Potatoes with Pesto Sauce

Ingredients   *6 servings*

2 cups dried lentils   4 potatoes, cubed

Pesto Sauce
2 cups fresh basil, chopped   a few sprigs of parsley and thyme
6 garlic cloves, minced   salt and pepper to taste
1/2 cup olive oil

1. Preheat oven to 350°.

2. Wash and drain the lentils. Boil them until they are tender. Drain.

3. Meanwhile, boil the potatoes in a separate saucepan. They must remain firm and not overcooked. Drain.

4. Blend the pesto ingredients in a food processor or blender until smooth (add more oil if necessary).

5. Thoroughly butter a deep baking dish. Place the lentils and potatoes in it. Add the pesto sauce and mix well. Bake for about 20 minutes. Serve hot.

"Put your hands to work and your hearts to God, and a blessing will attend you."

—Mother Ann Lee, Shaker sister

Ragout of the Harvest

Ingredients   *4–6 servings*

1 onion, chopped
olive oil
6 tomatoes, peeled and sliced
4 garlic cloves, minced
1/3 cup mixed fresh herbs, chopped
   and minced (parsley, basil, thyme)
1 bay leaf

2 cups white wine or vermouth
6 potatoes, sliced
4 carrots, sliced
1/2 pound lima beans
   (or 1 package, frozen)
1 zucchini or yellow squash, sliced
salt and pepper to taste

1. In a large saucepan, gently sauté the onions in the oil until they begin to turn golden. Add the tomatoes, minced garlic, herbs, and bay leaf, and cook for about 5 minutes, stirring from time to time.

2. Stir in the cup of wine or vermouth and cook a minute or two. Add the potatoes, carrots, and lima beans. Cover the pan and cook over low or medium heat until the vegetables are tender.

3. Add the zucchini or squash and continue cooking for another 8 minutes. Season to taste and add more wine if needed. When the ragout is ready, it should rest with the lid on for at least 5 minutes before serving. Remove the bay leaf. Serve hot.

NOTE: This vegetable stew is a special treat at harvesttime, when the abundance of the garden can easily be transplanted to the table.

"He who sees things grow from the beginning will have the best view of them."

—Aristotle

Soybean Casserole

1 cup dried soybeans
2 onions, sliced
2 garlic cloves, minced
1 carrot, sliced
1 celery stalk, sliced fine
1 cup spinach, chopped
1/2 cup parsley, chopped

10 ounces tofu, cut in cubes
4 tablespoons vegetable oil
2 tablespoons soy sauce
1 cup water
salt and pepper to taste
grated cheese of choice

1. Rinse the beans and soak in water. Drain. Cover the beans with fresh water and bring to boil. Skim off the foam that forms on top of the water and reduce the heat. With the saucepan covered, cook the beans for about an hour and 45 minutes, or at least until the beans are soft and tender. Stir from time to time so that the beans do not burn at the bottom.

2. Preheat oven to 300°. Thoroughly butter a large baking dish that has a cover. Place the beans and all the other ingredients, except the cheese, in the dish. Add the water and mix well.

3. Cover the dish and bake for about 1 hour. Uncover the dish, sprinkle on the grated cheese, and return to the oven for about 5 minutes, until the cheese melts. Serve hot.

"The grand essentials to happiness in this life are something to do, something to love, and something to hope for."

—Joseph Addison

Zucchini Loaf

Ingredients   *6–8 servings*

4 medium zucchinis, sliced
1 large onion, diced
1 green pepper, diced
1 sweet red pepper, diced
4 garlic cloves, minced
minced herbs (fresh parsley,
   thyme, basil)

2 eggs
1/3 cup milk
8 slices whole wheat bread
2 eggs, hard-boiled and mashed
salt and pepper to taste
olive oil

1. Gently sauté the sliced zucchinis, onion, and peppers in olive oil in a large skillet. Remove from heat, add the minced garlic and herbs, and then cover the skillet.

2. In a large, deep bowl, beat the 2 eggs and the milk together thoroughly. Add salt and pepper and continue beating. Slowly crumble the bread slices into the bowl, add the well-mashed hard-boiled eggs and the vegetables. With greased hands, mix and blend the contents of the bowl thoroughly and form into a large round ball. Refrigerate it in the bowl for at least 2 hours.

3. Preheat oven to 350°. Press the zucchini loaf into a well-buttered pan. Bake for 25 to 30 minutes. Remove from the pan immediately.

NOTE: This attractive and easy-to-prepare vegetarian dish may be served either hot or cold.

"Establish yourself in God, and then you will be helpful to others."

—Saint Seraphim of Sarov

Spicy Rice-Vegetable Casserole

Ingredients   *6–8 servings*

3 tablespoons butter
1½ cups rice (uncooked)
½ green pepper, chopped
1 onion, chopped
2 garlic cloves, mashed
3 carrots, sliced
3 large stalks celery, sliced

½ teaspoon thyme
½ teaspoon oregano
  (adjust to your taste)
salt and pepper
1 cup canned chickpeas,
  drained (optional)
3½ cups boiling water

1. Preheat oven to 350°.

2. In an ovenproof dish with a lid, melt butter; stir in rice so that all grains are coated. Add remaining ingredients and mix thoroughly.

3. Stir in the boiling water. Cover. Bake for 1 hour. You may wish to add 1 cup of heated chickpeas during the last 10 minutes.

"Whatever a man possess over and above what is necessary for life, he is obliged to do good with, according to the command of the Lord who has bestowed on us the things we possess."

—from the Short Rules of Saint Basil

Risotto

(seasoned rice)

Ingredients *6 servings*

1 onion, finely chopped
1 carrot, finely chopped
2 stalks celery, finely chopped
oil of choice
1½ cups rice

2 to 2½ cups broth or bouillon
2 teaspoons thyme
salt to taste
½ cup white wine
grated cheese (Parmesan is best)

1. In a large frying pan, gently sauté the onion, carrot, and celery in the oil. Add rice, 2 cups broth, thyme, and salt.

2. Cook over medium heat. When the mixture begins to stick to the pan, add the wine. Continue cooking until the rice is tender. The mixture will dry out as it cooks, so keep adding broth or bouillon to maintain moistness. If the rice is a variety that cooks quickly, you may have some broth left over. If, however, you use brown rice or another longer-cooking variety, you may have to add more broth or bouillon. Stir only to prevent sticking and when adding liquid. Otherwise, let simmer.

3. Sprinkle with grated cheese just before serving in a covered bowl that has been previously warmed.

"Mutual forgiveness of each vice
Opens the gates of paradise."

—William Blake

Indian Curried Lentils

Ingredients   *4 servings*

1 pound dried lentils
1 cinnamon stick
a few peppercorns
2 onions, sliced
4 tablespoons margarine

1 tablespoon curry powder
3 1/2 cups canned whole tomatoes
salt to taste
eggs, hard-boiled (optional)
shrimp, cooked (optional)

1. In a large pot, cover lentils with water and boil with cinnamon stick and peppercorns until lentils are tender. Drain and remove peppercorns and cinnamon stick.

2. Sauté onions in margarine, and then add other ingredients. Stir and heat through. Two quartered hard-boiled eggs or cooked shrimp may be added. Serve hot.

"Love a man even in his sin, for that is the semblance of divine love and is the highest love on earth."

—Fyodor Dostoevsky

Hudson Valley Codfish Cakes

Ingredients   *16–20 small cakes*

4 cups flaked codfish   2 eggs, well beaten
7 to 8 medium potatoes   1 medium onion, grated
1/2 to 3/4 cup milk, scalded   salt and pepper to taste

1. Cover fish with cold water and bring to a boil; drain.

2. Cook potatoes and mash. Add scalded milk and beat well. Add eggs and onion, and continue beating until mixture is creamy. Stir in flaked fish.

3. Form into balls, press flat, and fry lightly on each side. Serve hot.

"Solitude and prayer are the greatest means to acquire virtues. Purifying the mind, they make it possible to see the unseen."

—Saint Seraphim of Sarov

Eggplant Omelette

Ingredients

Ingredients   *4 servings*

1 small eggplant, thinly sliced   6 eggs, beaten
3 garlic cloves, minced   1 teaspoon cornstarch
1 large onion, sliced   1/2 cup milk
1/4 cup oil of choice   salt and pepper to taste

1. In a large frying pan, fry eggplant, garlic, and onion gently in oil until they are cooked (about 5 to 10 minutes).

2. Beat the eggs. Make a paste by mixing cornstarch and a little milk; add remaining milk and mix well with the eggs and seasonings.

3. Pour egg-milk mixture over the cooked eggplant and cook as an omelette. Serve immediately.

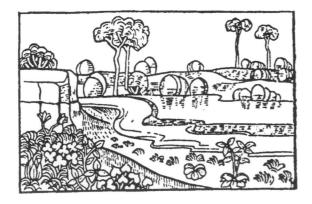

"And when we find ourselves in the place just right, it will be in the valley of love and delight."

—Shaker hymn

Roman Gnocchi

(Gnocchis à la Romaine)

Ingredients   *4 servings*

2 cups milk
dash nutmeg and salt
3/4 cup farina

2 eggs plus 1 yolk, beaten slightly
2 tablespoons butter
1 cup grated cheese, Italian preferred

1. Scald milk with nutmeg and salt. When just at boiling point, sprinkle in farina while stirring. Keep stirring as farina thickens. Turn off heat, beat in eggs, then add 1/2 cup cheese.

2. Pour into an 8-inch square pan and smooth surface so thickness is even. Chill thoroughly.

3. Preheat oven to 425°. Cut the cold gnocchi into squares, diamonds, etc. Place on an ovenproof, buttered platter. Dot butter on top; sprinkle with remaining cheese. Bake for 10 to 15 minutes.

"We are meant to believe through all darkness that God is love and only love, and to try to live by that faith alone."

—Mother Maria

Red Cabbage, Apples, and Onions

Ingredients — *6–8 servings*

butter
1 medium head red cabbage
8 apples, peeled and sliced
6 onions, sliced

1 bottle of red wine
1 bay leaf
salt and pepper to taste

1. Preheat oven to 350°. Thoroughly butter an ovenproof casserole (with a lid). Layer the cabbage leaves, apple slices, and onions. Repeat the layers until you finish.

2. Add the red wine, bay leaf (inserted somewhere in the middle), salt, and pepper, and cover the casserole. Place it in the oven, and cook slowly for 1 hour. Remove the bay leaf and serve. (This can also be served as a side dish with eggs, fish, or meat.)

"As I see it, we shall never succeed in knowing ourselves unless we seek to know God…."

—Saint Teresa of Avila

Kasha Salad

Ingredients   *4–6 servings*

4 ounces kasha
2 stalks celery, finely chopped
1 green pepper, diced
1 red pepper, diced
4 medium tomatoes, chopped
1 medium onion, chopped

1/3 cup fresh parsley, finely chopped
6 tablespoons olive oil
   (add more according to taste)
2 tablespoons lemon juice
salt and pepper to taste

1. Cover kasha with boiling water in a large saucepan. Simmer for 10 to 15 minutes, covered. Drain thoroughly and refrigerate the kasha for 1 hour.

2. Place the kasha with the diced and chopped ingredients in a deep salad bowl and mix thoroughly. Combine the olive oil with lemon juice and pour over the salad. Toss. Adjust seasoning. Serve cold.

NOTE: This nutritious and pleasant salad is good any time of year, but especially when tomatoes are ripe and sweet.

"Love God's young creation, love it as a whole and every grain of sand in it. Love every leaf, every ray of God. Love animals, love every plant and everything. If you love everything, the mystery of God will be revealed to you in things….And finally you will love the whole universe with a comprehensive, all-embracing love."

—Fyodor Dostoevsky

String Bean Salad

1 pound string beans
1 red onion, thinly sliced

1/3 cup fresh parsley, finely chopped
leaf lettuce

Vinaigrette

8 tablespoons olive oil
2 tablespoons white vermouth
2 tablespoons lemon juice

salt and pepper to taste
egg, hard-boiled and sliced (optional)

1. Wash and trim the string beans, and if they are especially long, cut them in half. Cook for 15 minutes in boiling water, rinse them with cold water. Drain thoroughly.

2. Add the onion and parsley. Prepare the vinaigrette according to directions on page 151; pour over the salad and mix well.

3. Arrange lettuce on individual plates with string beans on top. Garnish with slices of hard-boiled egg if desired.

"Prayer is the outcome of love, it is a form of love, it is therefore creative since love is the very life of God himself. The nearer anyone draws to God, the nearer he draws to all that God loves, that is, to the whole world and every single person in it."

—Sister Thekla

Three-Color Coleslaw

Ingredients   *6–8 servings*

1/2 small head green cabbage, shredded
1/2 small red cabbage, shredded
4 large-size carrots, peeled
   and shredded
1 small red onion, shredded
7 tablespoons low-fat mayonnaise

2 tablespoons lemon juice
1/2 teaspoon spicy or mild mustard
salt and pepper to taste
shredded mint leaves as
   garnish (optional)

1. Shred the vegetables by hand or with the help of a food processor. Place them in a large-size bowl.

2. In a separate bowl, mix well the mayonnaise, lemon juice, mustard, salt, and pepper.

3. Pour the mayonnaise mixture over the shredded vegetables and toss well. Refrigerate for 2 hours before serving. Serve cold.

"I like the fact that 'listen' is an anagram of 'silent.' Silence is not something that is there before the music begins and after it stops. It is the essence of the music itself, the vital ingredient that makes it possible for the music to exist at all."

—Alfred Brendel

Bessarion Avocado Salad

Ingredients   *4–6 servings*

3 ripe, firm avocados
3 tomatoes, seeded, sliced in cubes
1 cucumber, seeded, sliced in cubes

2 green peppers, seeded,
   sliced in circles
1 red onion, sliced

Vinaigrette
1/3 cup olive oil
3 tablespoons lemon juice
fresh cilantro leaves, chopped

fresh parsley, chopped
salt and freshly ground pepper to taste

1. Cut the avocados in half and discard the pits. Peel and slice them carefully lengthwise. Place them in a deep salad bowl. Add the remaining vegetables.

2. Prepare the vinaigrette by mixing and blending all the ingredients in a blender according to directions on page 151. Pour the vinaigrette over the vegetables, toss the salad gently, and serve.

Saint Bessarion was one of those early desert monks who lived in the Egyptian desert during the second part of the fourth century and was renowned for his extreme humility. He seems to have been an itinerant monk, a sort of vagabond for the lore of God, moving from place to place in the desert because he believed the Christian does not have a permanent home here on earth. He was also well known for his love of the poor, and one day when he had nothing to give to a beggar who requested his help, he went and sold his only possession, a book of the gospels, and gave the money he got for it to the beggar. When later he was asked about it, he responded, "I sold the book where it is written: 'Sell all that you have and give to the poor.'" Such was the faith and holiness of those early monks.

Pasta and Mozzarella Salad

Ingredients

8 ounce fusilli or penne pasta
1 roasted red pepper, sliced julienne
style (or a 7-ounce jar of the same)
1 bunch of fresh arugula, trimmed

5 ounces smoked mozzarella,
cut into small cubes
1 small red onion, sliced julienne style

Salad Dressing

6 tablespoons olive oil
2 tablespoon balsamic vinegar
1 tablespoon lemon juice

2 drops red pepper sauce
salt and freshly ground pepper to taste

1. Cook the pasta following the directions on the package. When the pasta is cooked, rinse it under cold water and drain. Place the pasta in a large salad bowl. Add the remaining ingredients: the roasted pepper, the washed and trimmed arugula (one may substitute watercress if arugula is not available), the mozzarella, and the onion.

2. Prepare the salad dressing in a small bowl, mix well, and pour over the salad. Toss the salad and serve. This salad may be served room temperature or cold after 1 hour in the refrigerator.

"Just as water when it is squeezed on all sides shoots up above, so does the soul when it is pressed hard by dangers often rise to God to be saved."

—Saint John Climacus

Pudding Délice

Ingredients   *4–6 servings*

1/3 cup butter
1/4 teaspoon salt
1 cup sugar
2 eggs
1 tablespoon vanilla extract or cognac

1 1/3 cups flour, sifted
3 teaspoons baking powder
1/2 cup milk
fruit (optional)
whipped cream (optional)

1. Preheat oven to 350°. Cream the butter, salt, and sugar. Add the eggs and vanilla or cognac. Beat well. Add the flour and baking powder alternately with the milk, and continue beating.

2. Pour the mixture into a buttered casserole dish and bake for 35 to 40 minutes, until the pudding sets. Allow the pudding to cool, then cut in squares. Serve with fruit and whipped cream.

"Though the saint knows the mountain of God's love from having lived on its heights, the pilgrim in the valley can at least see the mountain and appreciate its grandeur from the distance. He or she can call out to other pilgrims and tell them of life lived on the heights."

—Peter Kreeft

DESSERTS

Saint Bruno's Coffee Cream

(Crème au café Saint Bruno)

Ingredients   *4–6 servings*

1 quart milk
2 tablespoons instant coffee
2 teaspoons coffee extract
   or coffee liqueur

6 egg yolks, well beaten
1/2 cup sugar

1. In a heavy saucepan, combine the milk, instant coffee, and coffee extract or coffee liqueur. Bring almost to boil while stirring constantly.

2. Combine egg yolks and sugar in a mixing bowl; beat thoroughly. Slowly pour the hot milk into the egg mixture while continuing to beat with the mixer. It must be thoroughly blended.

3. Return the mixture to the saucepan and cook over low to medium heat, stirring continually until the cream begins to thicken. Just before the mixture reaches the boiling point, remove from heat and pour into bowl. Stir once or twice, cover, and refrigerate until serving time.

Saint Bruno was the founder of the order of Carthusian monks in the eleventh century. Born in Cologne, he taught theology at the Rheims Cathedral school. Later he withdrew with six companions to the wilderness of the Grande Chartreuse. There he built hermitages and established the Carthusian monastic way of life, which combines solitary and communal life. In a letter to an old friend, he spoke of the great beauty of that way of life: "Only those who experience it can know the benefit and delight to be had from the quietness and solitude of a hermitage."

Peaches with Strawberries "Monte Cassino"

(Pêches aux fraises Mont Cassin)

Ingredients   *6–8 servings*

10 ounces strawberries

3 pounds peaches

4 tablespoons strawberry jam

1 cup fruity white wine

1 cup sugar

1. Wash and trim the strawberries. Dip the peaches in boiling water, cool, and carefully peel and cut in perfect halves. Pit. Refrigerate with the strawberries.

2. Combine the jam, wine, and sugar in a heavy saucepan. Simmer over low heat, stirring constantly, until sugar dissolves and mixture thickens into a syrup. Cool.

3. When it is time to serve the dessert, slice strawberries. Place peach halves on dessert plates, fill hollows with sliced strawberries, and pour the syrup on top.

"Monks should practice zeal with ardent love. They should anticipate one another in honor, most patiently endure one another's infirmities, whether of body or soul. Let them try to outdo each other in obedience. Let no one do what is best for himself, but rather what is best for another."

—from the Holy Rule of Saint Benedict

Cold Spring Rice Pudding

(Riz aux oeufs)

Ingredients   *8 servings*

1 cup rice
1 cup boiling water
3 cups milk
3 eggs
$^1/_2$ cup sugar

1 teaspoon vanilla
pinch of nutmeg
$^1/_2$ cup to 1 cup raisins (optional)
1 teaspoon cinnamon (optional)

1. Combine rice and boiling water. Cover and let sit 40 minutes, or until water is absorbed. (Rice will be partially cooked.)

2. Preheat oven to 350°. Beat together all other ingredients. Put rice in a deep buttered baking dish; pour egg mixture over it. Bake for 40 minutes, or until custard is set.

"God wants us to sing alleluia and to sing it truthfully from our hearts without any sour notes from the singer. Let us sing alleluia with our voice and our heart, with our mouth and with our life."

—Saint Augustine

Saint Placid's Pumpkin Chiffon Pie

Ingredients

1 cup sugar

1/2 cup milk

2 cups canned pumpkin

3 egg yolks, well beaten

1/3 tablespoon salt

2 teaspoons cinnamon

1 teaspoon vanilla extract

1 envelope plain gelatin

1/4 cup cold water

3 egg whites, beaten stiff

Pastry Shell

2 cups flour

1 stick sweet butter

1 egg

5 tablespoons ice water

pinch salt

1. Prepare the pastry shell according to the instructions on page 156. Bake until done; cool.

2. Combine the sugar, milk, pumpkin, egg yolks, salt, cinnamon, and vanilla in a saucepan. Cook slowly over low heat, stirring constantly and mashing any lumps until the mixture thickens and becomes smooth.

3. In a large bowl, soften the gelatin in the cold water. Slowly add the pumpkin mixture, stirring constantly. Set the bowl in ice water to cool. When the mixture is cool and begins to congeal, fold in beaten egg whites. Pour the pumpkin mixture into the baked pie shell and chill for at least 4 hours.

Saint Gregory's *Dialogues* charmingly narrates how Placid became one of Saint Benedict's first disciples in Monte Cassino and how he was saved from drowning by the prayers of the holy patriarch. Saint Benedict had a particular affection for the young Placid, since the child was entrusted to his care. Saint Placid's feast was celebrated until recently on the fifth of October, hence his name on a harvest dish.

Quick Apple Cake

(Gâteau aux pommes)

Ingredients

2 eggs

1/3 cup milk

2 teaspoons baking powder

6 tablespoons sugar (white or light brown)

3/4 cup whole wheat flour

small pinch salt

1/3 cup oil

4 apples, peeled, cored, cut in 1/4-inch slices

1/2 cup cream or condensed milk

1 teaspoon cinnamon

1. Preheat oven to 350°.

2. Butter an 8-inch baking pan. Beat eggs well; add milk. Combine dry ingredients, except cinnamon, and add to egg mixture; beat in oil. Batter should be quite thick.

3. Spread batter in pan. Arrange the apple slices on edge over entire surface. Bake 15 minutes. Remove from oven and pour cream or condensed milk over surface and sprinkle with cinnamon. Return to oven for another 25 minutes.

"As we progress in our monastic life and faith, our hearts expand and we run the way of God's commandments with unspeakable sweetness of love. Thus, never departing from his school, but persevering in the monastery until death, we may by patience share in the passion of Christ and deserve to have a share also in his kingdom."

—from the Holy Rule of Saint Benedict

Appendix

Sauce Béchamel

Ingredients   *about 2 cups*

2 tablespoons butter or margarine   1 tablespoon dry sherry (optional)
2 tablespoons cornstarch or flour   pinch of nutmeg (optional)
2 cups milk   salt and pepper to taste

Melt butter or margarine in a stainless-steel pan over low to medium heat. Add the cornstarch or flour and stir with a whisk. Add the milk, little by little, until smooth, continuing to whisk. Add the sherry, salt, pepper, nutmeg, and continue stirring. When it begins to boil, reduce the heat and cook slowly until it thickens.

This sauce is excellent for use with fish and vegetables, and a necessary base for soufflés, some omelettes, and other egg dishes.

Sauce Mornay

Ingredients   *about 2½ cups*

2 cups of Béchamel sauce   4 tablespoons grated Gruyère cheese
  (see preceding recipe)   10 tablespoons heavy cream
4 tablespoons Romano
  or Parmesan cheese

When the Béchamel sauce is at the boiling point, add the cheese and let it melt as the sauce thickens. When the sauce is smooth and thick, withdraw it from the heat and add the heavy cream while stirring continually with a whisk or a mixer.

White Sauce

Ingredients   *about 1–1 1/2 cups*

2 tablespoons butter or margarine   salt and freshly ground black pepper
2 teaspoons cornstarch or flour   nutmeg (optional)
1 1/2 cups milk

Dissolve the cornstarch or flour in 1/2 cup milk. Melt the butter or margarine in a stainless-steel pan over medium heat. When it begins foaming, add the milk mixture, stirring continually. Add the rest of the milk, salt, pepper, and nutmeg, and stir until the sauce comes to a boiling point. Lower the heat and continue stirring until the sauce thickens. The sauce is ready when it is smooth and thick.

This sauce can be used as a basis for many other useful variations. It can be used on fish, meats, eggs, and vegetables.

White Sauce with Herbs

Prepare a white sauce. Add 3 tablespoons of finely chopped fresh herbs (tarragon, dill, parsley, thyme, etc.) and 1/2 teaspoon dry mustard. Mix thoroughly.

White Sauce with Mustard

Prepare a white sauce and stir in 1 teaspoon of French or dry mustard.

Hollandaise Sauce

1/2 cup melted butter
3 egg yolks
1 tablespoon fresh lemon juice
1/2 teaspoon salt

1/4 teaspoon white pepper
dash of nutmeg
1/3 cup boiling water

Whisk the melted butter with a mixer while adding one egg yolk at a time. Add the lemon juice, salt, pepper, and nutmeg, continuing to whisk with the mixer. Just before serving, place the bowl in a saucepan with 1 inch boiling water, or in the upper part of a double boiler. Over low heat add, little by little, the boiling water to the sauce while stirring continuously, until the sauce thickens.

This sauce can be used on fish, veal, egg, and vegetable dishes.

Tomato Sauce

Ingredients   *about 2–2½ cups*

6 tablespoons olive oil

1 large onion, finely chopped

3 garlic cloves, minced

2 pounds tomatoes, skinned and sliced

3 tablespoons tomato purée

1 carrot, grated

4 tablespoons fresh basil, finely chopped

1 bay leaf

salt and pepper to taste

pinch of thyme

Heat the olive oil in an enamel or stainless-steel saucepan and sauté the onion and the garlic slowly for a few minutes until they are soft and transparent. Add the rest of the ingredients. Lower the heat and simmer for 30 to 40 minutes, stirring from time to time. While the sauce is cooking, partially cover the saucepan. When cooking time is complete, turn off the heat and let the sauce rest a few minutes before serving. Good on pasta dishes and egg dishes.

Pesto Sauce

(Sauce au pistou)

Ingredients   *about 1½ cups*

4 garlic cloves, minced
½ cup fresh basil leaves, finely chopped
⅓ cup pistachio nuts, finely chopped

6 tablespoons grated Parmesan cheese
1 cup olive oil (or more)
pinch of salt

Mash the garlic and basil with a mortar and pestle. Add the pistachio nuts and continue mashing thoroughly. Place the mixture in a larger container, gradually add the olive oil, cheese, and salt, and blend thoroughly.

A simpler and quicker way to prepare the pesto sauce is to place all the ingredients in a blender and process as smooth as you wish.

This sauce is usually used with pasta, but it can also be used with gnocchi, seafood, eggs, and vegetables, such as zucchini.

Mushroom Sauce

1 ounce butter or margarine

1 onion, finely chopped

$1/2$ pound mushrooms, chopped

1 cup sherry or white wine

$1/2$ teaspoon ground turmeric

$1/2$ cup fresh parsley, finely chopped

salt and freshly ground pepper

Melt the butter or margarine in an enamel or stainless-steel saucepan. Add the onion and cook until transparent. Add the mushrooms, wine, turmeric, salt, and pepper, and cook until the mushrooms begin to turn brown. Reduce the heat, add the parsley. While stirring, cook thoroughly for another 4 to 5 minutes, until the sauce is done.

This sauce is excellent on top of rice, fish, meat, and eggs.

Simple Vinaigrette

(Vinaigrette classique)

Ingredients   *about 1/2 cup*

1 teaspoon salt   2 tablespoons wine vinegar
1/2 teaspoon freshly ground pepper   6 tablespoons olive oil

Place the salt and pepper in a cup or bowl. Add the vinegar and stir thoroughly. Add the oil and stir until all the ingredients are completely blended.

Vinaigrette with Garlic

(Vinaigrette à l'ail)

Prepare a simple vinaigrette, adding 1 minced garlic clove. Let the vinaigrette stand for a few hours before using.

Vinaigrette with Herbs

(Vinaigrette aux herbes)

Prepare a simple vinaigrette, but replace the vinegar with equivalent lemon juice. Add $1/4$ cup finely chopped herbs (parsley, tarragon, coriander, scallions). Mix thoroughly.

Vinaigrette with Mustard

(Vinaigrette à la moutarde)

Prepare a simple vinaigrette, adding 1 teaspoon Dijon mustard.

Sauce Mayonnaise

1 egg yolk
1 teaspoon mustard
2 teaspoons lemon juice
  or tarragon vinegar

1 teaspoon salt
$1/_2$ teaspoon white pepper
$3/_4$ cup light oil or canola oil

Place the egg yolk in a bowl, add the mustard, salt, and pepper, and begin to mix with a whisk or a mixer. Add the oil, a little at a time, then lemon juice or tarragon vinegar, and more oil, continuing to mix until the mayonnaise thickens. Keep the mayonnaise in the refrigerator until it is ready to be used.

The mayonnaise can be used for hard-boiled eggs, potato salad, Russian salad, or on asparagus, etc.

Sauce Aioli

Prepare a mayonnaise as indicated above. Add 5 minced garlic cloves. Mix thoroughly and refrigerate the sauce for several hours before using. This sauce can be used on seafood, salads, vegetables, and cold meats.

Tarragon Sauce

(Sauce à l'estragon)

Ingredients   *about 1 cup*

1/2 cup sour cream   salt and white pepper to taste
3 tablespoons lemon juice   3 tablespoons chopped tarragon
1/2 cup heavy cream

Place all the above ingredients in a deep bowl and with a mixer stir and blend thoroughly. Refrigerate until ready to use on salads, seafood, etc.

Fine Dough for Tarts and Quiches
(La pâte brisée)

Ingredients   *1 pie crust*

2 cups flour
1 stick lightly salted
   butter or margarine

pinch of salt
1 egg or 2 yolks
5 tablespoons ice water

1. Work the flour, salt, and butter or margarine together with the fingers by rubbing lightly. When texture is even, pour egg and water into well in the center. Using a finger, stir the liquid quickly into the flour, starting at the inside and gradually moving to the outside. Gather the dough up into a ball. Cover with a well-wrung-out damp cloth or foil, and put in the refrigerator to rest for 1 or more hours.

2. Preheat oven to 300°. When the dough is ready to be worked, sprinkle some flour over the table (or board-and carefully roll out the dough, extending it in every direction. Butter a tart or pie dish thoroughly and place the rolled dough into it with care. The dough must always be handled with the fingers. Trim the edges in a decorative fashion. Cover the pastry shell with aluminum foil and place in the oven for 12 to 15 minutes for a prebaking period. Refer to individual recipe for remaining baking instructions.

This recipe is basically to be used for salty dishes: quiches and vegetable or meat tarts.

Sweet Fine Dough for Fruit Tarts and Pies

(La pâte brisée sucrée)

Prepare a basic dough for tarts and quiches, substituting 1 stick of sweet butter for the salted butter and a pinch of sugar for the salt. You may also add an extra egg for a richer pie crust.

This recipe can be used for dessert dishes, fruit tarts, and pies.

Rich Pastry Dough

(a crunchy dessert shell)

Ingredients   *1 pie crust*

- 2 tablespoons pecans, finely mashed
- 2 cups whole wheat flour
- 1 teaspoon baking powder
- 1 stick sweet butter or margarine
- 1 teaspoon brown sugar
- 1 tablespoon vegetable oil
- 8 tablespoons ice water (more if needed)
- pinch of salt

Prepare the pastry shell by mixing all the ingredients and following the instructions given above for fine dough. The combination of whole wheat flour and nuts provides a splendid rich texture to the crust and gives a nut flavor to tarts and pies.

This crust is excellent for open tarts and pies.

Three Kings Brandy Eggnog

Ingredients   *5 cups*

1 egg yolk
$1/_2$ cup cognac
4 tablespoons sugar

4 cups milk
dash of nutmeg

Combine all the ingredients in a blender, and process until foamy. Refrigerate if not served immediately.

Honey and Molasses Drink

Ingredients   *2 glasses*

2 tablespoons honey
2 tablespoons molasses
1 cup water

1 cup milk
dash of nutmeg

Combine the honey, molasses, and water in a saucepan. Bring to a boil. Add the milk and nutmeg,
continuing to stir. Simmer for 2 or 3 minutes. Serve hot.

Mint Tea

Ingredients   *about 4 cups*

6 tablespoons mint leaves, chopped   2 inches orange peel
4½ cups water   sugar or honey to taste

Bring the water to boil and add the mint and orange peel; boil for 5 minutes. Simmer for 2 or 3 minutes more. Strain and serve the tea, and let each individual add sugar or honey according to taste.

Linden Tea

(Tilleul)

Ingredients   *about 4 to 5 cups*

8 linden leaves, including   5 cups water
   young sprigs and flowers   sugar or honey to taste

Bring the water to boil, add the linden leaves and sprigs. Boil for 5 to 8 minutes. Simmer for 2 or 3 minutes. Strain and serve the tea. Let each individual add sugar or honey according to taste.

Coffee, Vienna Style

2 egg yolks

4 teaspoons sugar

2 cups hot coffee (instant is fine)

2 tablespoons heavy cream

Beat each egg in the cup in which the coffee will be served. Add the sugar and mix thoroughly. Pour the hot coffee into each cup and stir. Add 1 tablespoon heavy cream to each cup. Stir and serve immediately.

Hot Chocolate

(Chocolat chaud)

2 tablespoons bitter chocolate

1 cup water

1 cup milk

2 tablespoons sugar

Bring the water to a boil. Add the chocolate and the sugar. Stir until they are totally dissolved. Add the milk and bring to a simmer. Simmer for 2 or 3 minutes. Serve hot.

These seasoning mixes are made with dried herbs and spices. If you wish to use herbs from your garden, dry them by hanging in bunches in an airy clean space, out of the sun. When crisp to the touch, crumble the herbs with your fingers, discarding the stems. Measure the ingredients for an herb blend into a bowl and rub together with fingers to mix. Store in airtight containers out of the light.

Bouquet Provençale

Ingredients

1 teaspoon thyme
1 teaspoon basil
1/2 teaspoon rosemary

1/2 teaspoon sage
1 bay leaf (use whole, remove
   before serving food)

This can be used for vegetables, sauces, and meat.

Apple of My Eye

(Prunelle de Mes Yeux)

Ingredients

1 teaspoon dry mustard
1/2 teaspoon sage
1/2 teaspoon thyme

1/2 teaspoon white pepper
1 teaspoon chives

This can be used for vegetables, meat, and grains.

My Spices

(Mes Épices)

Ingredients

3/4 teaspoon parsley flakes   1 teaspoon tarragon
1/2 teaspoon onion powder   1/4 teaspoon paprika
1 teaspoon sweet red pepper   1/2 teaspoon lemon flakes

This can be used for vegetables, seafood, and sauces.

Mixed Herbs

(Herbes Mélangées)

Ingredients

1/2 teaspoon garlic powder   1/2 teaspoon oregano
1/2 teaspoon marjoram   1/2 teaspoon sage
1/2 teaspoon thyme   1/2 teaspoon chives

This can be used for vegetables, sauces, and poultry.

Index of Recipes Using
Fresh Fruits and Vegetables

Index of Recipes

Addresses of Monasteries Where Food Products Can Be Purchased

"Ora et Labora" is the motto of the monasteries that live under the *Rule of Saint Benedict*. For centuries, contemplative monks and nuns have supported their lives of prayer and praise to God with manual labor, an essential part of daily monastic life. Monastery food products are known internationally for their quality and their long tradition of excellence. Products can be purchased directly from the small monastery stores or by mail.

Abbey of the Genesee
3258 River Road
Piffard, NY   14533
585-243-0660, ext 27
www.monksbread.com
(variety of monks' bread and cakes)

Abbey of Gethsemani
3642 Monks Road
Trappist, KY 40051
800-549-0912
www.gethsemanifarms.org
(Trappist cheese, fudge, and fruitcakes)

Abbey of Regina Laudis
The Monastic Art Shop
273 Flanders Road
Bethlehem, CT 06751
www.abbeyofreginalaudis.com
203-266-7637
(culinary herbs, vinegars, jams, jellies, cheese)

Holy Cross Abbey Monastery Bakery
901 Cool Spring Lane
Berryville, VA 22611
540-955-9494; fax 540-955-4006
www.monasteryfruitcake.org
(fruitcakes, truffles, honeys, fraters)

Monastery Greetings
540 East 105th St. #105
Cleveland, Ohio 44108
800-472-0425; fax 216-249-3387
www.monasterygreetings.com
(foods from several monasteries, including Our Lady
of the Resurrection Monastery)

Mount of St. Mary's Abbey
300 Arnold Street
Wrentham, MA 02093
866-549-8929; fax 215-922-1335
www.msmabbey.org
(candy)

Our Lady of Guadalupe Trappist Abbey
Mailing address: PO Box 97
                               Lafayette, OR 97127
Shipping address: 9200 NE Abbey Road
                               Carleton, OR 97111
503-852-0107; fax 503-852-7748
www.trappistabbey.org
(ginger date-nut cake, fruitcake, and honey)

Our Lady of the Mississippi Abbey
8318 Abbey Hill Lane
Dubuque, IA   52003-9575
866-556-3400 Fax 563-585-2343
www.trappistine.com <http://www.trappistine.com>
(Trappistine creamy caramels, mints,
chocolate coated caramels, chocolate and
vanilla caramel sauce)

Our Lady of the Resurrection Monastery
Barmore Road
La Grangeville, NY 12540
www.monasterygreetings.com
(cookbooks, wine vinegars, jams and jellies, herbs)

Transfiguration Monastery
Saint Benedict Shop
701 State Route 79
Windsor, NY   13865
www.transfigurationmonastery.org
607-655-2366
(salsas, jams, wine vinegar)

In France:
L'Artisanat Monastique
68bis Avenue Denfert Rochereau
75014 Paris
www.artisanat-monastique.com